Date Due

BRODART, INC.   Cat. No. 23 233   Printed in U.S.A.

GRANDMA MOSES

My Life's History

GRANDMA MOSES

MY LIFE'S HISTORY

Anna Mary (Robertson) Moses.

Edited by Otto Kallir

HARPER & BROTHERS, PUBLISHERS

CONTENTS

[v]

ILLUSTRATIONS

These reproductions in color of paintings by Grandma Moses will be found at the end of the book.

In Black and White

[vii]

PREFACE

When the first book on Grandma Moses was in the making,* the artist wrote a few pages of autobiographical notes, as well as comments on some of her pictures, which showed her amazing ability to express herself in her writing in that same simple and direct way so characteristic of her paintings. During the following years Grandma Moses was asked on several occasions to write brief sketches referring to various episodes and experiences in her life. She responded to these requests so readily, and her unpretentious stories were so well received that the idea suggested itself of asking her to write more of her "life's history," as she called it. The result is this book.

It may interest the reader to learn how the autobiography was written. Grandma Moses did not write it in chronological order. As mentioned before, the nucleus was the short notes she contributed to the first book on herself and her art. Two articles, published in the *New York Times* on May 11, 1947, and on November 21, 1948, followed; they were entitled "How I Paint and Why" and "Turkey and Trimans." Both were reprinted in modified versions to serve

* *Grandma Moses: American Primitive*. Edited by Otto Kallir. First edition Dryden Press, New York, 1946. Second edition Doubleday, Garden City, 1947.

as introductions for the catalogues of two shows held at the Galerie St. Etienne in New York. During the year 1949, Grandma Moses began to write more about herself. She started with her wedding and her first years of married life in the South, and then went on to tell childhood memories.

The material took shape and grouped itself into three parts. The first comprises her childhood, her very limited schooldays, and her life as a hired girl. The second begins with her marriage and migration to Virginia, and describes how she lived there with her family up to the time they returned to the Hoosick Valley in her home state of New York after an absence of twenty years. The third chapter covers the span from 1905 to the present day.

It was interesting to note how easily and gladly Grandma Moses recollected the smallest details from childhood and early married years, whereas it was difficult for her to write the third chapter. One hundred and thirty-two pages, entirely in her own handwriting, were devoted to the first half of her life, but she has given only thirty-seven pages to the second half, although it is this late period that has made her world-famous, bringing her, in 1939, at the age of almost eighty, the discovery of her talent as an artist and all the extraordinary events that followed.

When Grandma Moses visited in New York City in 1949, I questioned her on various topics and took down her answers on a tape recorder, as the writing in longhand had become too much of a strain for her. But we did not continue in this way for very long because Grandma did not feel at her ease with "those modern machines." Several supplementary parts, relating to all three chapters of the book, were then taken down from dictation at her home in Eagle Bridge, and that was the method she liked best.

After some repetitions, which resulted from this way of proceeding, had been eliminated, and the numerous sketches put in chronological order, the complete manuscript was read to Grandma Moses and her family; on this occasion some corrections were made.

Not a single sentence that is not by Grandma Moses has been added, so that the present volume is an authentic picture of the life of the artist, written and told by her in her own words. I had to make but one change upon the special request of Grandma: that was the occasional correction of her spelling.

The report on the way this book originated would not be complete without the grateful mention of the valuable help given by Hildegard Bachert, who, entering fully into Grandma Moses' intentions, undertook the task of writing down her dictation.

My thanks also go to the members of the Moses family for their understanding and co-operation while the work on the book was in progress.

OTTO KALLIR

New York, June 26, 1951

Childhood Days

CHAPTER ONE

WHAT a strange thing is memory, and hope; one looks backward, the other forward. The one is of today, the other is the Tomorrow. Memory is history recorded in our brain, memory is a painter, it paints pictures of the past and of the day.

I have been asked to recall my life's history, which with me is hard to do. I don't know how to go about these things. Some people can tell a story and make it very interesting, some make it very dry, just the way they express themselves.

But I will try to give you an idea of who and what I am.

I, Anna Mary Robertson, was born back in the green meadows and wild woods on a farm in Washington County, in the year of 1860, September 7th, of Scotch Irish ancestry.

My ancestors came to this country at different times between 1740 and 1830, all of them settling in the immediate vicinity of southern Washington County, New York State.

[3]

Here I spent the first twelve years of my life with mother, father and sisters and brothers. Those were my happy days, free from care or worry, helping mother, rocking sister's cradle, taking sewing lessons from mother, sporting with my brothers, making rafts to float over the mill pond, roaming the wild woods, gathering flowers, and building air castles.

I was one of a family of ten, my mother was one of eleven, my grandfather of fifteen, while my husband was one of a family of twelve children.

My Forefathers

My ancestors were early settlers in Cambridge. There was one of them that married an Indian girl, way back in the 18th century, there weren't many girls then. None of us children showed it, but I have second cousins here that show it very plainly. When once a man was boasting to me about his ancestors and that his folks came over in the Mayflower, I told him, "You know, my folks were here to meet yours." Then he didn't boast any more about the Mayflower.

My grandfather's father on my mother's side came from Scotland, and his name there was Shonan. His grandfather, Joseph Shonan, and son, John Shonan, went to the Isle of Man as fishermen. It is a small island between Ireland and England. They lived with two brothers by the name of Roch, and a sister, Anastasia Roch.

After a time, John Shonan and Anastasia fell in love and wanted to get married. But as there was no priest or minister on the island, they had to cross over to Ireland.

They gave the priest their names, and he said there was no such name in all Ireland, and he named them John and Anastasia Shanahan. Now, if there is any property in Scotland, we could not claim it, as the name has been changed. I always disliked the name, and still dislike it. Probably it was customary to put *han* on Irish names, as they do *van* on Dutch names; I don't know.

John and Anastasia had four or five children. My grandfather, Gregory Shanahan, the eldest child, remembered, when a little child, of sitting on the floor and playing with his grandpa Shonan's silver buckles on his slippers. He must have died when my grandfather was quite small, as he did not remember him so well.

John and Anastasia both died with fever, when grandfather was eleven years old, leaving him to care for his sister and two or three brothers, as they had no kin there. He found homes for them with the help of the neighbors.

Then one of the neighbors gave him a loaf of bread, and in the dawn of morning he started acrost the country to find an uncle, his mother's brother, James Roch. He walked all day, and just before sundown he came to his uncle's home. But the uncle was dead. And the widow sat on a plow, and was weeping hard, with her three or four little children around her.

He told her who he was, and that he would plow while she went to the house and got something to eat. She had borrowed the horse for the day to plow her garden, but was so weak that she could not hold the plow but for a short time, and the garden was but half done. Grandpa plowed till dark, then took the horse home. But the neigh-

[5]

bor told him to come get the horse and finish the garden for his aunt.

He lived with her and helped to care for the children till they could do for themselves, probably about fifteen years.

When he came to this country, about the year 1836 or 1838, as near as I can tell, he came from county Waxford, Ireland, with his brother Sylvester, coming over on the same ship that grandma, Bridget Devereaux, her bothers, Peter and John, and a sister, Margaret, were on. They were six weeks coming over. John Devereaux was a sailor and paid their passage. The captain of the ship was a cousin by marriage to grandma, Captain Archibald Buchanan, a Scotchman. He had sailed in many waters.

Grandma and grandpa met on board ship first. Then, after reaching America, they both went to work. Grandma worked for a family in Waterford till she was married.

My grandma Shanahan was left an orphan in early childhood, with a sister and three brothers. The sisters were taken by an aunt, Bridget Senet, mother-in-law to Captain Buchanan. Mrs. Senet kept a store and the girls were a great help to her. For some time my grandma's duty was to go downstairs in the morning and take down the shutters and dust up the store.

The aunt had a talkative parrot. There was a very poor family acrost the court from the store, and sometimes, they did not have anything to eat, grandma would sneak a loaf of bread under her apron for them. One day the parrot told on her. Then her aunt forbid her to take any more bread.

Now there is something more of grandpa's life. When

he came to this country, he worked in Pittstown, New York, for some time, for fifty cents a day. But he saved up enough to buy himself a comfortable home, where he lived and died, about 1877. I think he had a fairly good education for his day. He went to night school in Ireland, while living with his aunt. He also had learned the shoe-maker's trade, so that he made all of his children's shoes. I have seen him at work on them. My mother has said that she was twelve years old before she had a pair of boughten shoes.

My great-grandfather, on my father's side, Hezekiah King, was born in Amenia, Dutchess County, New York, 1755. He was the son of Captain John King and Elizabeth Fenner King. When he was about twenty years old, he left his home and travelled into the Cambridge Valley, looking for a place in the wilderness, where he might build his future home, and there he cleared land and built him a house about 1778, it was destroyed in 1800 by fire. It was a shingled house, the sills were hewed about 8 or 10 inches thick, from 12 to 20 inches wide, the cellar walls still mark the site of the old home. He taught the first school in Cambridge. The town was born in 1773, it lies between the North line of the Hoosick Patent and Steven-son's Corners, now Coila. At the time the town was founded, Cambridge was a part of Van Rensselaer Patent, and covered all the territory now known as White Creek and Jackson, two beautiful valleys.

When his country was calling for soldiers, Hezekiah King enlisted in the 16th Albany County Militia, and marched to meet the British. He served at Ticonderoga, there he carved his powder horn, it is still there and bears this inscription:

Hezekiah King. Ticonderoga. Feb. 24th 1777.
Steal not this horn for fear of shame,
for on it is the owner's name.

Here in this valley he built a church, so it was called the King Church Valley.

Hezekiah King had six daughters, and each daughter had a child. His oldest daughter, Sarah, was my grandmother on my father's side. One day in 1822, great-grandpa asked them all home, and he would give a dress to the grand-child that he thought the smartest and prettiest. So they all came home with their babies. By and by, when they were all talking, little Russell (my father) disappeared, but where—no one knew. So a search was sent out, and he was found up in one of the large chambers. But how did he get there? His little nurse was accused of taking him there, and for punishment was told she could have no pie for dinner. Russell was brought back and left on the floor, he was creeping and forgotten about. By and by great-grandpa saw something disappearing through the cat hole in the front hall. That was Russell, he was going upstairs again on another investigation. There he got the name Cat. In all well-made houses they would have cat holes in the hall doors, so that the cat could roam through the house. And also it was for the draft for the fireplaces. As you remember, there would be two or three large chairs by the fireplace with high backs and a foot stool for the feet to keep them out of the draft.

Father was chosen the finest baby and got the dress, but

[8]

aunt Celina said her baby had ought to have got the prize, as he was a large fat baby. . . .

My father's other grandfather was Archibald Robertson, born in Scotland in 1748, came to this country about 1770, coming to the Cambridge Valley, and located on the hills west of Coila. He was a wagon maker by trade. He built the first wagon that ever ran over the Cambridge pike, building it with an ax and saw. In later years he made the best wagons between Boston and Buffalo. He was a Presbyterian by creed, somewhat of a musician and a believer in second sight. His oldest son was my grandfather, William Archibald Robertson.

My father had an older brother, Archibald. Some would say he was cracked, but he was smart and shrewd. When he was young, he learned striping the wheels of the buggies and put a monogram or whatever people wanted on the side of the buggies. He was an expert at this work and made a good living with the painting business.

When they first commenced to talk about bicycles, Archibald Robertson thought he could make them as good as the boughten ones. He got a big wheel, pretty high, and made a bicycle of it. He could balance himself on that wheel, but he forgot to put on any brakes. He started out to come down this long hill, he got to going so swift that he didn't dare to get off, and the farther he went, the swifter he went, and when he got nearly to the bottom, he ran into the side of the barn, breaking the clap-boards of the barn off. The wheel went in, but he stayed out on the ground. He never tried the bicycle any more.

He once predicted that the day will come when there are going to be wagons running over these roads big

[9]

enough to carry a load of potatoes, and there will be no horses drawing them. People said, he was "dippy in the dome," but wasn't he quite a seer!

My great-aunt, Celina King, told me those stories. She was the youngest daughter of Hezekiah King and lived in the King Church Valley on the Hezekiah King homestead. She had raised a family of five children and several grandchildren, but they were all grown and gone, and aunt Celina was living alone in a new house she had built on the old homestead property. Her husband died when the youngest son was two years old. In those days it was a real struggle to raise a family, with the head of the house gone, but aunt Celina, though a very small woman, was very determined in a lady-like way and raised a lovely family.

My father, Russell King Robertson had a flax mill near Greenwich, where I lived when I was small. He was a farmer and inventor, a dreamer, a believer in beauty and refinement. He was a kind neighbor, a help to all that knew him, a great instructor to us children, a kind and helpful husband.

Now this has been to give you insight into my forefathers' families.

From the Kings I got art, from the Robertsons inventive faculty, from the Shanahans thrift, the Devereaux generosity.

Now, to Go On about Myself

I was named in a casual manner when I was a child, but father didn't like it. My mother's sisters were Anne and Mary, one wanted to call me Anna and one wanted to call me Mary, so they doubled the name. And mother said, "It would be all right if you call her Anna Mary, I do detest the name Mary Anne." But father didn't like the name, he always wanted me called Sarah after his sister, so I was called Sissy until I was about six years old. About that time, a man came into the yard one day and wanted to know what my name was, and what was my little brother's name. I said my name was Sissy and brother's name was Bubby. So I didn't know what a name meant up until that time. I told mother what this man had said, and she told me then what my name was.

You see, they didn't pay much attention to the kids. But they thought a lot of their kids anyway, I don't know but that they didn't think more of them then, than now. Mother didn't go to bed that she didn't go around to see that they were all sleeping and covered up, and father watched over us too.

❖

We were five boys and five girls at home. Lester was the oldest boy, then Horace, then I, and then Arthur. Probably mother lost some babies, there is a vacancy after Arthur. Then came Celestia, Miama, Ona and Joe, then there was a lull, then Sarah and Fred. We came in bunches, like radishes. I was older than all the sisters. Arthur and I were like chums till he died. Arthur ran alone before I did. I was too heavy in the sit-down. We were about of the same size and not so far apart in age. We kind of went off by ourselves. Arthur and I would talk and sympathize with each other. I remember one time in the spring of the year we sat in the grass and talked about how pretty things were, and he said, "almost as pretty as heaven!" But, he said, "When I get to heaven, I want lots of good things to eat," and I says, "I don't care for the good things to eat, but I want lots of flowers, when I go to heaven."

Many a time I had to rock the cradle; I liked it, but I had rather been outdoors with my brothers. The four of us were always together. I always had to be one better than they. If Lester climbed the eaves of the house, I would go up to the peak. It was a strife with me to out-do them. But Lester could swim, and I couldn't! Father tried to teach me, but the minute he took his hand away—down I'd go! I was too heavy, like a polly wolly.

❖

Things that I do remember, away back in 1863.

I remember of walking down the road with my mother and father to the brook where they watered the horses, and I would run ahead of my two brothers, so as to pick up little birds. They were little grey birds with small bodies and long legs and very swift on their legs, and as they ran, their tails would tip up; I think they were called "tip-ups." I would pick them up into my little pink apron, but as soon as I put them in my apron, they would run out the back of it; I never could get my apron full of them. But my brothers could never catch one, mother said it was because I was swifter on my feet.

In those days father and mother lived away back in the green fields, and Sundays father would take us for a walk, and mother would go if the day was nice. Father

[12]

would carry the baby (as there was most always one). There was no other entertainment but to go to church, so it was a walk for a change. If we had visitors, they would go with us, and one time mother's sisters went with us, and one had a very pretty "jockey." That was a straw hat with flowers and ribbons hanging down the back. They were worn by young ladies in those days, all bright colors, and I did want one so *bad*, I cried, so she took it off and put it on my head. Well, that would have been fine, but mother said I was not a big lady for crying. Then I and brothers ran on ahead around by the mill pond. I had forgotten my "jockey" and when I put my hand up, it was not there, and someone said it must have blown into the mill pond. That was terrible. Don't think I've liked water since.

Then we went down by the raceway, and I wanted to walk on it to the mill, because brother Lester did, and father said, no, must stay in the road with brother Horace. We went through the flax mill, and father hung up the steelyards which he had to have to weigh his flax with. He put a strap around us small fry and hung us up to weigh us. I wanted to stay in the strap, so that I could swing, and mother said, no, we were going down by the woods and maybe get some whipper wills shoes. I liked those, to me they were so pretty, but that day we did not find any.

I don't remember coming back, think someone must have carried me.

Aunt Ruhama

The year of 1860, Aunt Ruhama lived in Lone Jack, Missouri. Her father had gone out there the year before to help them to build a mill and had died with a fever. Then her husband died that fall, leaving her all alone with three children, Charlie, Isabella and Arthur, cousins to me. Then the war was on, and Aunt Ru had the mill and a store across the road from her house. There was fighting all around them, and the Southerners were burning all the buildings, so to get all the deserters for the Southern Army. Then they set fire to her mill and store. She put the fire out twice that day, but the general told her it was no use to try to save it, it was his orders, and they must burn the house. She begged him to spare it for one more day, and would he watch over it for one day. Then she went some miles to get an old man to come with a one-horse wagon and take her twenty miles to the train so that she could go home. The old man came, and she put all she could on the wagon, then she got in. She had on large hooped skirts and carried little Arthur on her lap, the little girl on her knees in front, and her son Charlie was on the wagon floor, curled around her feet, so that he was hid, as he was 13 and tall for his age, and if they had caught him, they would have taken him into the Southern Army. The old man would walk so as to make the load lighter. Then once in so many miles a soldier would stop them to see that they had not concealed someone on the load, but they did not look under her hoop skirt. But one soldier ran his bayonet through her bed tick on the back of the load. Thus they travelled the twenty miles. Then she paid the old man, and he went back, and she came on alone to her mother's home in New York State. They burned her mill and store when she was gone. Father had her come and live in his tenant house, which she did for the following years. It was nice to have her and the cousins.

The Burning of Our Mill

One day in May, Lester, Horace and I ran away. It was early in the morning, and we hurried out of sight, we ran for aunt Ruhama's house. Father was acrost the pond; he did not see us. When we got to Auntie's, she was washing. She had the tub on two chairs, half full of soap suds, and was rubbing the cloth on a rubbing board, and the suds foamed up white like snow. They were so pretty, I climbed up on the round of the chair to play in them. The cousins were playing in the doorway, when all at once aunt Ruhama threw up her hands and said, "Oh, Russell's mill is on fire!"

She wiped her hands on her apron, caught hold of my hand and said, "Come children!" and we ran out, shutting the door, and up over a hill, and my legs got so tired, and Auntie would say, "just a little further." We got to the barn and met mother. She had seen the smoke, and she told Lester to run to the house and get all of the water pails, and for me and Horace to go to the house and stay with aunt Libby, or we would all be burned up. I remember crying and seeing the valley all full of smoke.

Well, aunt Libbie rocked me to sleep, and I knew no more till supper time, and mother came in, and her dress was all wet, as she had been carrying water.

[15]

How well I remember that old mill and the cupola on top, that I was always a'going to have for my doll's house, and the mill men with their smutty faces, all covered with flax dust. I was really afraid of them.

A few years later father had built a new mill.

❖

Once we were going to Cambridge to have our photographs taken. Some people in the tenant house wanted to go, so father, mother and my three brothers all went to have ours taken. Lester had a suit with a garibaldi waist and long pants; I in copper toe shoes, pantalettes, a garabaldi dress, that was banded in the waist, full-gathered dress and sleeves, like a shirt waist. Horace would not shut his mouth (probably had a cold), and Arthur cried, he was afraid. It was when they put your head in a vice, so that you would hold still. We went in the old red sleigh and the two horses, Bill and Fan. Father and mother had their pictures taken, but did not want to, as they were dressed in their workaday clothes. It was a happy day.

Then, when we all got home, the house was cold, and mother told us to keep on our coats till father built the fire, which he did with flax shives. They make a very hot fire. We burned them by the bushel in those days.

❖

Spring came, and I and brothers would run in the meadows to gather flowers. The first was the arbutus, that some-

[16]

times grows under the snow, then Indian moccasin, and those starry ones, we used to call pinks, they were all colors, white, purple, dark blue, and then there is some that are striped.

Mother always had a flower bed. When uncle John was there one summer, he helped her, so he could raise his own tobacco. That's all the tobacco I ever seen raised. It is very laborious, probably on account of the help.

In the corner of a broken mirror we used to keep a vase with flowers always. We loved to pick 'em and bring 'em in, and then mother would have to come and throw them out. When the whipper will blossoms were out, we had to get them for sure, they were the prettiest things. They were like a pansy, only more dainty and longer in the blossom, a blue purple.

My First Thanksgiving

The very first Thanksgiving I remember was about the year of 1864. Father was going to Union Village to buy himself some boots, and he was to buy me a red dress. I was to be a good girl all day, in hopes of getting a red dress. I tried to do everything I was told to do. But when candle-light came, father came in from the flax mill and said he could not get his boots, because it was Thanksgiving Day, and the stores were closed.

I was heart-broken, to think I did not get my red dress! I could not eat my supper. Mother said it was too bad, as I had been a good girl that day, but they never thought of the stores being closed.

Father patted my head and said, don't worry, as he was

going to Center Cambridge in a few days, and would try there; and so he did.

But the dress was not red, it was more of a brick red or brown. I was awful disappointed but said nothing. So I never got what I call a red dress.

I have found in after years it is best never to complain of disappointments, they are to be.

Death of President Lincoln

One day, mother, aunt Lib and I, we left Greenwich to come down to grandma's, just above Eagle Bridge where she lived. Mother was driving the buggy, an old fan horse, a gentle horse, and father let her drive it down. I don't remember the trip so much until we got down into Coila, and there I saw my first team of oxen, and I didn't know what they were. They were yoked together and were grazing along the side of the road. The grass was up and quite green. And I had to ask what they were and if they'd hurt you, all those questions. I will say I was about four years old, it was the first green grass I had seen that spring, and I wanted to pull off my shoes and go out and walk in it. And aunt Lib said, "Oh that wouldn't be lady-like."

Then we went on a little farther, and mother noticed that everything was trimmed in black. I remember her saying, "Oh, what has happened?" It was war times, and we got down in the middle of Cambridge, and she went into the store and asked what had happened. The pillars on the store were all wrapped in black bunting. And this man told her that President Lincoln was shot the night before.

[18]

And I remember her coming back to the buggy and she said to aunt Lib, "Oh, what will become of us now?" And if she hadn't used those words, I don't suppose I would have ever remembered it.

At Home

Generally Saturday afternoons everybody would take a bath. The tub would be brought into the kitchen, we had big wooden tubs, they held a lot of water. The children would take their bath in the afternoons, when they had more time. After supper they would go right to bed. The grownups took it after supper before they went to bed.

We felt better after the bath, and father would say, "Got all the scurf skin off?" Father would wash his feet every night before he went to bed. He believed in that.

Of course, they always washed their faces and hands and arms when they were doing dirty work. Father, when he came in from the mill, his beard always would be full of dust, and he always had to wash it. His hair was cropped right in back of the ear. That was the style of that time. He had a very good, strong nose, and that peculiar blue eye, it was a dark blue. I never see him but when his hair was grey.

We never heard anything about brushing teeth. I suppose they didn't need it as much as we do now, because all the food they ate was coarse. Not so much cake, and half the cake they did have was made with corn meal. That may be the reason why they had good teeth. My

[19]

brother Lester never had a toothache and never had a tooth pulled. When he was in his eighties, he could crack a hickory nut as fast as he could eat them.

❖

My parents didn't believe in whipping. Once we had company, and I was not permitted to sit down at the table. Arthur was younger than I, but he could sit at the table, and I didn't like that, I wanted to sit at the table, and mother said, "No, you'll be a lady and wait with me." And I started to bawl, and father told me to stop crying, and at that I cried more and more, just as loud as I could holler, and father said, "If you don't stop, I will take you to the shop and whip you!" Grandpa was there, and he was quite stern and said, "Children should be seen and not heard," and father got up and took me by the arm and took me out to the shop. The shop floor was full of long, curly shavings, and he picked up one of those shavings to whip me with, and that made me mad, I stamped my foot, and I shouted, "If you strike me with that, I will never like you again!" I was in a regular tantrum. I can see father look down at me now—and he had this long beard—and I could see this smile under the beard, as much to say, "You little imp." He led me back to the table, and someone put a plate down for me on the table, I expect they had finished eating. He didn't even touch me with the shaving. The first time you lift them, they'd fall to pieces, he was just trying to scare me.

That's the only time I remember of him trying to cor-

Russell King Robertson, Grandma Moses' father, about 1860

Margaret Shanahan Robertson, Grandma Moses' mother, at the age of twenty-four

At the age of four   At the age of fifteen

THE TWO EARLIEST PHOTOGRAPHS OF GRANDMA MOSES

rect me in any way. I was his favorite, if he had a favorite,
I was the girl among the three boys.

❖

1865, my first Fourth of July that I remember, father
had been over to Greenwich the day before and bought
some firecrackers and torpedoes and nigger-chasers for us
children. The next morning, the Fourth of July, Pa gave us
our share, but the nigger-chasers were for mother and
had to be kept till night. Then we were to clean out the
kitchen, place the chasers on the floor and touch a match
to them. They would chase each other all around the
kitchen floor, spitting fire at each other; they looked
like snakes.

I had a nice pink apron with two pockets in it; mother
had made it. She did all the sewing by hand in those days.
And that morning father filled my pockets with torpedoes.
They were about the size of marbles, twisted up in a
piece of very tough paper, filled with stones, powder and
so forth, and when you threw them on something hard,
they would go off, making a noise like a pistol.

I and my three brothers had lots of fun that day. We
had our first peanuts, the first we had ever seen. We thought
them wonderful. We ate the shell and all, they tasted kind
of toasted and good.

❖

I liked to play mother and dolls. We used to cut out paper
dolls, we didn't have much of anything else. I had the

[21]

greatest row of dolls, and I would invent dresses for them. I also would color their faces. Mother used to buy indigo and tie it up in cloth to make her blueing. So I got into mother's blueing. I got that for the eyes; some grape juice, if I could get it, for the lips, and have very pretty dolls. I took pleasure in getting a whole row of them, see which is the prettiest of all of my dolls. They all had to wear corsets. And my brother used to get them sometimes, and oh, he used to pull them to pieces. We fought with our tongues. He'd say hateful things, and I would say hateful things, I suppose. I also made petticoats for my dolls. I spent my time that way, until the baby started crying. Then I'd go down and rock the cradle and attend to him. The dress, I would have with trimmens on it. The trimmens were flounces, in those days they'd wear flounces. On the nicest dresses I would have maybe three flounces. My petticoats were scalloped, because mother had scalloped skirts. Colored paper and white dolly was very pretty. Sometimes I got lots of trimmens, when I got hold of some colored paper. Or father would give me an orange colored envelope. Otherwise everything was white or newspaper. Once, grandma Robertson came, and she brought some tissue paper, green and pink and those colors. Oh, I was rich when I got that! Grandma was a wonderful good woman bringing me that!

❖

One summer there was a little girl in the tenant house, and we got up in the yard or in the orchard and built houses. We would get a nice spot and pick up the largest stones and build a room, and that would be surrounded by stones, and finally we'd have three or four rooms. We would each have a house. Hers would be a little different than mine. Then we would get hold of broken dishes, and we would have a pantry with shelves, and we would set our dishes on them. All imagination! Then we'd get our dolls and our sun bonnets and we'd go visiting each other.

Mother thought it was so foolish, why didn't I spend my time knitting, or why didn't I crochet? I didn't like to. Mother tried to teach me to knit, but I couldn't hold the needle, and I took a dislike to it. It was hard work. I couldn't bother with that. But I could knit lace, and knit different patterns of lace. When I got along in my teens, I knitted quite a lot of it.

When I was a child, everybody knitted their own stockings, there was no boughten. Mother always had a knitten in her pocket. She knit very fast. When I was maybe 12, 14 years old, they'd begun to get stockinettes. It's just like the ribbing on the top of the stocking. You would buy it by the yard, all colors. All you'd do was to cut it off in sections and sew up the toe. My mother used to buy a good many yards of it, pink, brown, lavender; for the women folks you would most always have lavender. Then you could get it in wool, and they would have the bright colors. So that did away with a lot of knitting.

A Thunderstorm

My first thunderstorm was in 1867. That had been a very hot, dry summer in Washington County, New York. I remember our well went dry and father trying to locate a spring and of him digging three different ones to get pure drinking water, and seeing the neighbor's cattle going around the fences bellowing and father saying they would die of thirst, and of my brother going and telling the neighbor that the cattle had no water.

This Sunday it was very dry and warm, and the pond had nearly dried up, and mother said she would like to see it. Father, or Pa, we used to call him, said he would carry the baby if she thought she could walk. Then I was happy, as I always wanted everybody to go where I went. As we went by the mill pond, it was about one third full with water, and so many fish in it, but one half of them were dead for want of fresh water. Pa said, "What a pity," and if it didn't rain soon, he would have to get them out and bury them the next day. I can see them now, lying all around the edge of the pond, with their white bellies.

Well, we went on down by the flax mill, and brother Lester said he heard it thunder. So we went up over the hill back home. When we got on top of the hill, we could see a dark cloud all acrost the north, and father said, "There is a hard storm over Bald Mountain, 15 or 20 miles away, and it is coming fast!"

Mother hurried to the house to close the windows, and aunt Maria went to shut up the chickens. Father and the hired man shut up the barns. Then Pa hurried to the house, the hired man said he would stay in the barn.

Father had no more than got into the house, than here came the wind. It struck the tree tops and bent them to the ground, sweeping the yard clean. Then the rain came down in sheets. We thought the windows would break in, and mother told us to keep away from them.

I saw father take his coat and wrap it around the baby, Miama. He was holding her, and he said, "If the house goes, run to the little orchard and get hold of one of the trees

[24]

and hold your face against it, they are young trees, and the roots will hold!"

The water came in on all the sides of the house. But the storm did not last long. Then father and mother commenced to sweep out the water; it was about three inches over all of the floors.

The hired man, his name was Jim Buck, had stayed in the barn. He said he got into the buggy and sat down. But as soon as the storm struck the barn, it blew both doors open and blew him and the buggy right out acrost the drive into the orchard!

The brook that ran through the meadow in front of the house was like a river. The pond was bank high, and the fish were all gone.

There was a beautiful field of corn acrost the pond, but the storm had washed a gully through it, a gully so deep that a man could ride on horseback in it, out of sight. The earth that had washed out of the gully was red. Father took that soil, it was so very fine, like baking powder, he sifted it and washed it and used it for paint. He painted many a barn with it, and it is still on them now, it was decayed iron ore. The rain continued for several days, all wells and springs were filled. "No great loss without some small gain," Pa said.

That was the worst storm I ever saw in my childhood days.

❖

The first time I ever knew that there is such a thing as a birthday was when I was seven years old. My brother and I were out in the orchard, in the black cherry tree. We nearly lived in that tree, as the cherries were just right and nice. This day mother called me into the house—I supposed, to rock the cradle. But she said, "Anna Mary, do you know how old you are?" I didn't know about being old, I hadn't heard about any such things. "Well, today you are seven years old." And then she went on and told me how we had birthdays. She told me that "today is your seventh birthday." "What does that mean?" I wanted to know. It meant that I had been in the world for seven years, she said.

The First of My Painting

When I was quite small my father would get me and my brothers white paper by the sheet, it was used for newspapers. He liked to see us draw pictures, it was a penny a sheet and it lasted longer than candy. My oldest brother loved to draw steam engines, that was a hobby with him, the next brother went in for animals, but as for myself I had to have pictures and the gayer the better. I would draw the picture, then color it with grape juice or berries, anything that was red and pretty in my way of thinking. Once I was given some carpenter's red and blue chalk, then I was rich, children did not have so much in those days, we appreciated what we did get.

Father was not well that winter, he had pneumonia. One day he said to mother, "Margaret, how would you like me to paint the walls?" And mother said she did not care, just so they were clean. So he commenced in one corner of the room and painted a scene he had seen the spring before up at Lake George. It was so pretty, mother told him to do some more, so he painted different scenes all around the room. That was a lasting wall paper. When he was painting, we tried to get into the paints, trying to paint something; just little scenes mostly. Underneath the clock shelf there was a square space, and father told aunt Maria she could have that to paint a picture on it. She was along 40, 50 years old. I did not like the picture she'd painted, I could do better than that, and I commenced to paint on sticks of wood. Next summer I would get pieces of slate and window panes. Then I had some pretty pictures. That was the time they made fun of me, I had some "very pretty lamb scapes," as my brothers said I called them, they had some brilliant sunsets, and father would say, "oh not so bad." But mother was more practical, thought that I could spend my time other ways.

❖

That Thanksgiving mother's sister came to spend the day. After dinner aunt Sophia put the wish bones over the door to catch a fellow she said, but "what was a fellow?" I wanted to know, and she laughed at me saying "It is just as well you don't know."

She was a very pretty girl and was going to Chicago, that was a long ways off in those days, and I felt bad, it was the first parting I have ever realized.

❖

We had a very deep snow that year, and while it was falling, father would hitch up the horses to the old big red sleigh and break out all of the roads, as we lived back in the fields, probably half a mile from the main road, and father had to keep the road open. He would drive up to the kitchen door, and we would all climb into the sleigh onto a lot of straw and blankets, and away we would go, out to the main road, then on through the woods, and oh! that was grand to drive under the hemlocks and have the snow fall on us! Then back home and around the barn, back to the house. Oh, those happy days!

Then the sun came out and melted the snow on top, and then it froze so hard, it would almost hold up a horse. It was so cold, my brothers could not go to school, and we played on the crust on the snow. We would go up a field above the orchard, get on our sleighs, and away we would go! Lester had a sleigh with cast iron runners, Horace had an old wash bench, upside down, but very safe, Arthur a dust pan, and I an old scoop shovel. Oh, what fun! We would play out for hours, and the thermometer at 25 below zero.

Sugaring Off

The snow all went off in February, and father tapped the maple trees, and we made a lot of syrup and sugar. We children would have to run to the trees in the early morning and gather up all the sap that had accumulated during the night and then again in the afternoon and again just before dark. Sometimes it would run much faster if it was thawing than at others. Sometimes it would freeze up, and we would have to wait a day or two before it would start running again. Towards the last of the run the sap seemed to have soured, and then we would have to abandon it. The sap was boiled down two-thirds away in a large arch kettle outdoors in the day time, then at night it was finished off in the house on the cook stove.

That was a pleasure for us children to run to the woods to gather the sap and run back with it, and we had lots of fun keeping the fires burning. We all had all the syrup we wanted to eat on buckwheat cakes in the morning and syrup on hot biscuits for supper with butter. Then for drink we would have sweet fern tea, that was maple sap boiled down to a certain degree with sweet fern. With cream it made a very nice drink, and father would say it was healthy, a blood purifier. You had to cultivate a taste for it, but it was very nice, and father let us have all we wanted of it.

I never got into sugaring-off parties, they came on later than my day, further up in Vermont it was an old custom. Younger ones would have a gay time, they'd pour the syrup when it was just ready to turn to sugar on dishes of snow for each to eat; they would eat their fill and go home to dream sweet dreams.

❖

That spring father got all of his plowing done in March, his oats sowed, the frost was all out and the ground settled. We children were allowed to take off our shoes and boots, the birds had all come back, and on the thirtieth of March father drove away to go to what is Valley Falls now. He said he might not be back that night, and we children were to do the work at the barn, such as feeding the sheep, cows and horses. Mother would do the milking.

It was a beautiful morning, but before noon it commenced to cloud up and got very cold, and that night it commenced to snow, and by morning there was two feet of snow on the ground. It was so cold, mother put on father's boots to go out to milk the cows, and Lester put on one of father's coats and took along some warm corn for the hens. They did up the feeding, or as they called it "the chores." Mother said when she fed the hens, a lot of birds flew down to eat with them, and there were dead ones everywhere.

Father did not get back till April first. He had to leave his buggy and borrow a cutter, that was a small, very light one-horse sleigh. He did not get a chance to return the cutter for ten days.

It was a cold, backward spring, for all the warm March. Almost everyone lost their oats, but as luck would have it, father's had not sprouted before the freeze up.

❖

My worst memory goes back to the time when I first commenced to realize what the world was like, and I used to worry. I remember one summer that my mother wasn't well, and we children were afraid she was going to die. I would go to bed at night and cry, afraid mother was going to die.

The first death I remember was a young man that lived in the tenant house. I suppose he had what was called cancer of the stomach. And mother had been down and sat with him all the day before he died. The day of the funeral she told me that I should go down and go in to see him. That's the first dead person I have ever seen. I probably was about eight years old. My mother went in to look at him, and his sister went in with us and took the pennies off of his eyes, and I thought that was the funniest thing. But since then I have heard them say, "Why, they'd steal the pennies off of a dead man's eyes." But she put them back again.

Candle Making

In my father's day they never should let the fire go out from one end of the year to the other. In some homes they didn't let their fire go out in forty years. When the fire did go out, they had to run to the neighbors' to get red hot coal for it, or start it with a flint.

In my early days my mother had sperm oil lamps. The burner had two wicks; they drew the candle wicking through the burners and would have two little lights, it was a double light then. Then the sperm oil got so expensive and scarce that mother used to use a great deal of candle light, and in the pantry they used to have what they called "sluts." They would take a big, old-fashioned copper penny and lie it in a little piece of cloth which was set right down in the saucer, and then you could use any kind of old grease.

The candles were made in the wintertime, so they would harden quickly. We always butchered one beef a winter,

[31]

every farmer would, and the fat from the beef is called tallow—the waste fat, that is—we also have the suet, but the tallow is waste fat. The tallow is dried out and saved to make candles with. The minute it come around cool weather, we commence to make candles for the following year. We thread the candle molds with candle wicking and then melt up some of the tallow and pour it from the top into the candle mold, so it runs down into the mold. Then we set it outdoors for it to harden. Generally, we would fill the mold twice a day, morning and evening, depending on how many molds we had. That would produce from one dozen to three dozen of candles, depending on the size of the molds. When they were perfectly cold, then we could cut off the wicks and pull out the candles. Then you pack them in a box and set them away for the next summer. The children and the hired girl and the lady of the house, everybody had a chance in it, depending on who was the most idle—the same as we washed dishes. It was tiresome for me, I'd rather be outdoors playing, but it was a necessary job, just like soap making.

Women's Work on the Farm

Always had to make a barrel of soap on a farm to last the year through. And that was made from all kinds of waste grease. If we fried meat, and it was greasy, we took a piece of paper or cloth, strained the grease and put it in the soap skillet. In the spring of the year, we started the leach going. That is the barrel of wood ashes. In the bottom there would be holes, and you would fill up the barrel with water for lye. After you got enough of that lye, you would pour it into a large kettle and pour in all your waste grease, setting the kettle over a fire and starting it to boil. As it boils, you either add more grease, more water or more lye, until it eats up all the grease you put in, and then commence and try your soap. You take out, say, a cupful of soap, and you try it with water. If it makes a nice, strong jelly, amber-colored, then it is right. Then they drain it out into a barrel for the year's use. That was the women's work. We were thrifty, nothing wasted, nothing lost.

The weaving and spinning came in my mother's days. The girls didn't get any education because they had all that work to do. The girls knit the stockings. The wool, right from the sheep's back, they had to spin it, then weave it or knit it, and the men, they had "pepper and salt" suits. To make that cloth, they always had to have one black sheep in the flock, and the wool from that sheep made black yarn, and they'd weave that in to make the pepper and salt cloth, and it would wear for a generation. In olden days they were called "freedom suits."

When I was a child, they commenced to buy everything, the cotton cloth, and linsy woolsy—that was linen and wool woven together.

They used to bleach and starch things more than they do today. They would wear longer. You would wash out the starch, and the piece was clean. Years ago they used to starch linen sheets, and you can imagine, that coarse linen, starched and then ironed—you could slide into the bed on one side and slip out the other! In the war of the sixties mother had quite a few flannel blankets, and she used those instead of sheets, hoping every day that the cotton would get less, it was 40 and 50 cents a yard, and she used up all of her linens. Linen, at first, wasn't white, it was a grey, but it would bleach out very white.

Schooling was in those days in the country three months in summer, three in winter; little girls did not go to school much in winter, owing to the cold, and not warm enough clothing, therefore my school days were limited, but I was kept busy helping at home, and the neighbors.

A New Dress

Winter came early in our home town that year. Probably this was the last of November, and one evening mother said, while we were doing up the supper dishes, "How would you like to go to the village and get yourself a new dress?" I thought that would be grand. Mother said, "Your Pa will stay home tonight and take care of the little ones. Lester will take us up."

So Lester went to the barns and hitched up Fan and Bill, the horses, to the old red sleigh, which had some straw in the back and over the seat a buffalo robe and blanket for our laps. It was a lovely ride over the snow. When we got to Carpenter's store, brother hitched the horses to the hitching post, mother watched, to be sure all was safe. Wherever they stopped along by the stores, they had hitching posts—now they have parking meters.

It was my first time to enter a store, and I was somewhat afraid and hung to mother's arm. Mother told Mr. Carpenter that I wanted to buy a dress. He placed on the counter two pieces of calico, one was black and white, the other was a cinnamon brown. I did not like the first piece, but mother said it would wear longer. But I liked the brown.

The next morning after breakfast, the dishes washed and put away, beds made and floors swept, I was told to spread out the table and to get out my new dress, while mother looked up my pattern. And I thought this will be fun. But when mother came with the pattern and showed me how to lay the pattern and pin it down, then to cut out the dress, when that was done, I breathed a sigh of relief. But that was not the half of it! Then I was to get my thread, thimble and needle and to commence to sew up the skirt, and that had to be back stitch, and all of the seams likewise. That was my first dress.

There was no sewing machine in my mother's house, all the sewing was done by hand. We had a woman come one summer, and she stitched up the boys' pants with a little machine that she screwed to the table. Lester wore his pants to school, and when he came home, the legs were all open on one side. It was a chain stitch, and mother had to sew them all over. (Since then I've made many a dress, and when I was 88 years old, I made myself a velvet dress, and that had to be sewed by hand.)

The Whitesides

Then began the hard years.

When twelve years of age, I left home to earn my own living as what then was called a hired girl. This was a grand education for me, in cooking, house keeping, in moralizing and mingling with the outside world. I went to live with a

[35]

family by the name of Mrs. and Mr. Thomas Whiteside, they were lovely people, while well along in years.

The Whitesides, way back, had married into the Robertson family, and they thought there was no one better than the Robertsons, and everyone akin to them must be all right. Mrs. Whiteside had had a shock, and was poorly, but it got better, so she was up again, and there was no one but her husband in the house, and she thought that a young girl would be all that she needed, and that she should get me, as she knew the family. I went against my father's wishes, as he thought I should go to school, but mother thought that I would soon tire of it and would soon be home again. Mrs. Whiteside got so attached to me that she would not give me up, and I remained with her as long as she lived.

The Whitesides treated me as though I was their child, in fact, they called me "child." He was "man" and I was "child" to her always. She didn't want anyone to come near her but me, "child" had to do everything. She was an awful nice woman. I suppose I had got so she would see me as her own child. I felt the same way.

They were Presbyterians by creed. On Sundays Mrs. Whiteside believed in doing up the work in the morning, but after eight o'clock the breakfast was over and the chickens were fed, and everything was supposed to be done up for the day. One of my duties was to drive the horse, "Old Black Joe," to church for them and place bouquets on the pulpit in the church and always remember the text.

The Whiteside Church was built by Phineas Whiteside, about the year 1800, as near as I can tell. It was patronized by many creeds, even the Quakers. It was built with wide pine planks running up and down, it stood on the side of a hill by the side of a large track of woodland, the fields sloping away from it down into a valley, where a stream of water flowed, called the Fly Brook.

The church was largely attended, I have seen as many as four hundred gather there for worship. There were few churches in the community in those days; thus it went on for many years. The fathers and mothers would be laid to rest in the old burying ground, and a younger generation took their place. The church is still standing, and in good preservation.

Going to church on Sunday, this was a pleasure in olden times. The man of the house would arise early, feed the stock, milk the cows, curry off the horses; yoke up the oxen, if in winter, to the long sleigh, placing thereon a bundle or two of straw, while the wife or mother prepared a hearty breakfast, and put up a good lunch, and helping to dress all old and young in their best, banking up the fire in the fire place for a warm room on their return from church. Now the father walks and drives the oxen, mother cuddles the little ones, and grandma and grandpa sit on the back of the sleigh and watch over the younger generation.

Now they have reached the church, what an enjoyment, here they can exchange the news of the week, hear from the sick and the well, and spend the day in prayer, thanksgiven and song, a day of pleasure and rest from drudgery.

If all was well in the neighborhood they would go home singing those songs, "Work for the night is coming,"

"Sweet by and by," and this was a great favorite, "The mountains of life." And now the younger generation prefers to go to the movies.

❖

One day Mrs. Whiteside told me, if I would read the Bible through that summer, she would give me a silver thimble. Now that was quite an inducement, a silver thimble! So I would read the Bible through, but there were lots of words in it I didn't know, so I would skip them and read on, and I would get the meaning of the words but I couldn't pronounce them. And I read the Bible all through, but didn't know much more about it than when I started, until November she went to Troy and brought me my silver thimble. I was very proud of it and always wore it, till it wore holes all through it, and then my knuckles got so bad that I could wear it no more, but I still got it.

Mrs. Whiteside always had me sewing. I had made that first dress before, which kind of sickened me, it had to be made all by hand, the calico, that was kind of hard to sew. She kept at me, and what I would sew, was mine. She had me sew long strips of cotton to make rucking for the next of my dresses. That had to be hemmed and had to be made so fine, finer than sewing on the machine would be. I got so I could do it.

And then, the cooking, three meals a day. And then she had a large flower garden, so I had the weeding and hoeing in the flower garden beds. It was a duty for me to do this work, she could not do it. I liked to sit down in the shade and pull the weeds out. I didn't have to hurry, took my time. I also had the washing, ironing and churning to do.

After Mrs. Whiteside was gone, the old Mr. Whiteside would not give me up and kept me as a housekeeper. He was a man in his seventies. I was just like a kid to him. If I did anything that he didn't think was just right, he would reprove me. A Mr. Abbott and wife were caring for the farm.

That Thanksgiving Mr. Abbott, knowing we were alone, had asked us to come there for Thanksgiving dinner.

It was a cold, clear morning. It had snowed a foot or more, so that we had to shovel paths; Mr. Abbott had to hitch up the horses to break out the roads around the place and leading to the Whiteside Church. He had bells on the horses, and it did sound very pretty on that cold morning. I was busy shoveling a path to the well. They never thought of having water in the house.

At noon Mr. Whiteside and I went to Mr. Abbott's. We had a large steak for dinner, roasted with gravy, baked sweet potatoes, mashed turnip and potatoes, cranberries, cucumber pickles, brown and white bread and butter, coffee and minced pie.

After dinner we all went over to the Whiteside Church, where the Reverend Henry Gordon gave a lovely talk on Thanksgiving. The church was warmed by wood fires, and the pulpit was trimmed with evergreens and oak bows with acorns on them, quite pretty.

Mr. Abbott took us home from church, we had our first sleigh ride for that year. It was lovely, tucked into the sleigh with buffalo robes, bells a' jingling, and then to enter our home so warm and cozy, with coal fires, surely we should have been thankful, and I think we were.

I was proud in those days, could get up such fine dinners

for Mr. Whiteside's friends who came from far off to see him. When the minister came, and I could bring out the fine linen and the china tea set and the heavy silver, then with hot biscuits, home-made butter and honey, with home cured dried beef, I was proud. But I sometimes now think they came for eats more than to see him.

I remained with him until his nephew took charge of the farm and house.

School Days

Then I came over to Eagle Bridge and I worked for my board at Mrs. Abraham Vandenberg's for two years. My parents lived in Easton at that time; soon after they moved to Oak Hill. The last year my brother Arthur came in the wintertime and also worked for his board. Old Mrs. Vandenberg was good to me and to my brother; it was just like home. Both of us went to school at that time. They had a Mr. Mosher as teacher. The school at Eagle Bridge was considered the best district school around here, it is the same school which my children, grandchildren attended and great-grandchildren now attend.

In my mother's day, if a woman could write her own name, that was all that was necessary. When my mother was seven years old, she commenced to go to school, she left school when she was eleven, then she went into housework, and from there she got married, and she was 21 when she had three babies. That way of living was a kind of education, but there is another kind of education young people want nowadays.

When my mother went to school, she had the "Historical Reader" (I think I have one of them here, now they are old and scarce). It was an old reader, and it would be hard work for you to read. She carried that the four years she went to school. You couldn't ask her a question in geography that she couldn't answer, and she was better than father in arithmatic, yet, he was better in history. It seemed to be natural for her; arithmatic was hard for him, and he never could spell, but he could talk, he was intelligent in all respects. Of course, her geography she had learned in school. In class, when they pulled down the map of, say, the United States, they'd sing their lesson, and the teacher would commence: "Today we will have a lesson of the mountains." She would point, or one of the scholars would, with a long round stick, and as she pointed, the whole class sang the song about the mountains. The next day they would have the lakes, I remember that she used to sing to us:

> Oh Winnipeg, dear Winnipeg, if you will be
>   my Bride,
> I'll take you down to Athabask and be your
>   Slave, he sighed.
> This so displeased Miss Winnipeg, she called
>   him a Great Bear,
> And at the Slave she threw the Salt and Toole
>   and all were there.
> She drove him to Shiboqua Lake, way down
>   in Mexico,
> To grind with Nicaragua, he asked to be her
>   Beau. . . .

and they would point to each lake, and that's the way she learned it, the rivers and the capitals too.

When I went to school, the teacher would give us maps

to draw, and I would make the mountains in my own way, the teacher liked them, and would ask if he might keep them. We'd have to tell the counties in all of the Eastern states, we didn't know much about the Western states, it was supposed to be wild country.

Every Friday we would have to make a speech, and my brother Arthur, he would get up on the platform in his short pants and a white shirt, like a man's shirt, to speak his piece. And this one he had was on "Dried Apple Pies." He made his bow and spoke:

> Apples on a cord were strung
> And from the chamber window hung,
> And there they served a roost for flies
> Until ready to be made into pies.
>
> Tread on my corns or tell me lies
> But don't pass me dried apple pies!

At home, we children would have to cut the apples up in quarters or eighths, to dry and keep all winter. We would have a strife who had the largest number of strings. They were hung in a dry place till they were used for pies, but most of the flavor was gone.

❖

One day Mr. Vandenberg came in and said, "School starts Monday, now if you want to go home and see your folks, you will have to go today." That was Saturday. "I will come after you Sunday afternoon. You go over to the depot and take the train to Johnsonville, and then you wait

[42]

for the train that goes to Easton, and you get up on that." But I didn't, knowing that the train would not go until six o'clock, I started out on foot. It was probably three miles to Oak Hill.

When I got home, father met me at the door and told me I couldn't come in, he says, "There is eight of us just gone to bed with the measles, you better go on up to your aunt Mary's." That was three miles further, and it was getting dark, and mother called out and said, "No, Russell, better let her stay and help you take care of us." So I went in to take care of them, and we were up, father and I, all night and all the next day.

Brother Fred was a baby then, about three months old, and he was hungry, and cried and kept crying, we couldn't stop him. Mother was quite sick with the measles. Father said, "He is hungry," so I went to the pantry and fixed him a coffee cup full of bread and milk, and I used a good deal of the top milk, with sugar on it. I set it on the edge of the stove to get it warm, then took him and wrapped a cloth under his chin and commenced feeding him that bread and milk. I fed all of it to him. He went off to sleep. He had never had anything but the breast milk up to that time. He slept all night and way into the next morning. About 9 o'clock I got worried and looked at him, and he seemed to be sleeping good. I began to realize I should not have fed him bread and milk, I didn't know but maybe I had killed him! When father came in about 11 o'clock, I asked him to look at the baby, which he did, and he said, "He is all right." I didn't dare tell him what I had done. He was still sleeping at about 3 o'clock in the afternoon, when mother said, "I wish you would bring me the baby, he hadn't ought to sleep like this." I went to the cradle and picked him up, but I didn't dare uncover his face. I put him down on the bed beside mother, and she lifted the netting off his face, and I didn't dare to look, for I feared he was dead. As she lifted the veil from his face, she said "Oh my goodness!" and then I knew he was gone! I turned to look, and his face was as red as red could be, he was all broke out in measles! Fred lives to be an old man, he is in his seventies now.

Brother Lester had come home with the measles two weeks before, he was the one that peppered us all with it. I had them too after a certain number of days. I had to send word over to Mrs. Vandenberg that I didn't know when I would be back.

Horace was the only one that had the after-effects. He got a cough and father couldn't stop the cough. That was the first time we had a doctor. But he couldn't do anything. The measles had settled on his lungs. He never got well again, he died when he was twenty-one.

After we finished up here at the Vandenberg's Arthur hired out to a man by the name of Cass, but Arthur was a frail person for farm work. This whole week it had been raining, and the sheets were not really dry, and Mrs. Cass put the damp sheets on Arthur's bed. He noticed it, but he was tired and went to sleep, but the next morning he woke up and had an awful cold, and a bad cough. Mother wanted him to quit work and come home, but he didn't come till December, when all the hired men would stop. Along in February he was taken sick, and the doctor said he had a fever and he should go to Colorado. There were two different doctors in Hoosick Falls that thought that was the best for him. So he left about the fifth of

March, that was an awful time of the year to go. He was homesick and sick, but he stayed there till August, he didn't like the country, and he was turning worse all the time. He didn't last so long after he came home, the cough never stopped. He was 21 when he died.

My sister Miama died when she was about 18. A heavy cold brought it on, she never could get rid of it. She lingered along for about a year.

So I lost two brothers and a sister in six years, the funerals were two years apart.

We had to take the bitter with the sweet always. Those children could have been saved nowadays. The doctor could not have done any good at that time. Mother was very matter of fact, and she said, "As you are born you must die," and father took it in that way too.

My First Fair

There was a time when I would look forward from one fall to another just to go to the fair, and summer picnics. Those were about all the recreations we had in those days, and we would work the year through saving our money and our clothing. The first fair I ever went to was the State Fair in the year of 1876, the grounds were between Troy and Albany. It was called a very nice fair, and I was invited by the president, a Mr. Edwin Thorne. We left South Cambridge on the 10th of September going as far as Johnsonville on the steam cars; this was the first time I had ever been on a train, and I was very car-sick before we reached Johnsonville. There we changed cars, and had to wait. I saw my father at the lumber yard and thought

I could go over where he was and ride home with him and stay home till the others came back, but then I thought, no! How would I look riding on a load of lumber on the highway? So I went on, but was car-sick no more. We reached West Troy about one o'clock and had a nice dinner; there were a lot of young people from out Galway. After dinner we all went down the street and crossed

```
┌─────────────────────────────────────────────────┐
│      NEW YORK STATE AGRICULTURAL SOCIETY.         │
│                      ──                            │
│   36th ANNUAL CATTLE SHOW and FAIR                 │
│                   ALBANY,                          │
│        September 11th to 15th, 1876.               │
│                   ──◆◆──                           │
│   LADY'S TICKET. (NOT TRANSFERABLE.)               │
│                   ──◆◆──                           │
│   ⦿DMIT  Anna Mary Robertson                       │
│        AT ALL TIMES DURING THE SHOW.               │
│                   EDWIN THORNE, President.          │
└─────────────────────────────────────────────────┘
```

the ferry to the fair grounds. The first building we went through was the flower building, and oh, was not that grand! We had a lovely flower garden at home, but not like that, oh it was so sweet, and delightful in there. We stayed there till sun down. The next morning we all went back to the fair and this time we went through the poultry house, there were all kinds of feathered fowls. We were greeted as we opened the gate, "How do, how do, Polly wants a cracker"; Polly could speak very plain, that was the first time I had ever seen a parrot. From there we went through the stove building, a long house not so wide, with plenty of light. All along one side were cast iron cooking stoves of every description, behind every stove was a cook

[46]

or chef and a table, and as you passed the stove, someone would pass out to you some of the food that they were cooking on or in that stove; sometimes it would be hot rolls nicely buttered, then the next stove hot ginger bread or pies, and so forth; we did not have to go home for dinner, nor could we eat all that we got, and everything was the best. Oh those were the days—no hot dogs or sandwiches, that one never knows what the contents is! From the stove building we went to music hall, a large octagon building full of musical instruments, there you could not hear yourself think, but it was grand. From there part of us went to see the stock, and the rest to see the horses on exhibition. I liked that where the ladies rode on side saddles with long skirts and jumped hurdles; the horse racing was exciting but I did not understand it. Take it all in all it was three delightful days.

The Old Oaken Bucket

In the year of 1877 I was working for a Mrs. David Burch at what was called South Cambridge. One day after dinner, when the housework was did up, we thought we would go out and gather some wild strawberries. Mrs. Burch was an old lady, and she said, "I would like a drink of water." So I went to the well and drew up a bucket of water, and we drank of it.

Mrs. Burch said, "Anna, do you know what well you are drinking from?" I said, "No, I guess it is just a well," and she said, "This is the well of the old oaken bucket," and then, as we went to the strawberry field, she told me the story:

[47]

Back in the 18th century her great-grandfather lived in this place. He had an older brother who in his boyhood days fell in love with one of his neighbor's daughters. But her parents did not want her to go with Paul Dennis, as he and his people were poor folks. Well, that made trouble, and the young folks would write letters to each other, and they used one of the apple trees for a post office, and would sly out at night and exchange mail. Then Paul went off for three years as a sailor, in those days one had to sign up for three years, and Paul was young and got very homesick, and wrote the verses of the "Old Oaken Bucket." Then, when the three years were up, he came back to Boston and gave them to Woodworth, who set them to music, and therefore claimed them. There was no law against that in those days.

Then Mrs. Burch went on to tell me how one day, when she was very little, her great-grandfather took her hand, and they went to husk corn. He had around his shoulders a dode, they call it, a sort of a cape, and a gun in his hand. They walked over the bridge where the cataract fell, on to the field of corn. Then her great-grandfather spread the cape on the ground for her to play on, and gave her an ear of corn for a doll. By and by a large bear came down from the wild woods and commenced to eat the mound of husked corn, and she was afraid and crawled under his arm. But great-grandfather said, don't be afraid, as the bear would eat what he wanted and go back to his babies. She must have gone to sleep, for the next she remembered, she saw the old bear going back to the woods. It was an ugly sight, she said. She did not remember going back to the house, she thought her great-grandfather must have carried her.

She never knew why he had taken her with him that day, nor why he took the gun, unless he intended to shoot the bear, but having her with him, he dared not.

And now, all of this, the mill, the old shingled cot, the house, the wide spreading pond, is pasture land, the bridge and rock gone, the dairy house is now a store room. Then, the Johnsonville Railroad followed the brook bed up to Greenwich, and it was an old saying, anything that was crooked was as crooked as the Johnsonville Railroad. It was so crooked that the conductor could talk with the caboose man as they went around a bend. The railroad was put there to carry potatoes to the South, and now that it is gone, there is a state highway for trucks to haul milk.

In the springtime of life there is a plenty to do. Oh, those damp snowy days, early in spring, when we loved to go to the woods, and look for the first bloom of the trailing arbutus, which sometimes blooms beneath the snow, or gather the pussy willows. Feeling nearer to God's intentions, nearer to nature. Where in some respects, we are free, where there is beauty and tranquillity, where we sometimes long to be, quiet and undisturbed, free from the hubbub of life.

Haying time on the farm, when they gather the grain, fruit and berries of all description, and the little folks gather the eggs. When the church picnic comes, and the children can have all the cake and lemonade they want, water melon and peanuts, what a wonderful treat!

And the fall of the year, and there are many odd jobs to attend to, food to be stored away for the coming cold weather, the ground to be plowed for rye and other crops before it is frozen hard. Ditches to dig. Poultry to cull and house.

Thanksgiven, in some homes there will be rejoicing, in others there will be sorrow. But we, that can give thanks, should, there is so much to be thankful for, and praise God for all blessings, and the abundance of all things.

And then wintertime! When zero stands at 25 or 30, when we cannot deny the pleasure of skating till we have bumped heads, and bleedy noses, and the ice is like glass. Oh what joy and pleasure as we get together, to go for the Christmas tree, what aircastles we build as we slide down the hill, who can rebuild what we see on that Christmas tree.

Oh, those days of childhood!

In the South

Thomas Salmon Moses as bridegroom

Grandma Moses as a bride in 1887

Grandma Moses with her youngest children, Anna and Hugh, about 1904

Winona, Forrest and Loyd, Grandma's three oldest children

CHAPTER TWO

Thomas

THE fall of 1886 I went to a Mr. and Mrs. Sylvester
James to do house work and care for his wife, as she
was an invalid, and there were small children to look after.
I had been with them the year before, at that time they had
a hired man by the name of Tom Doill.

That evening when I got there, little Arthur James
caught hold of my hand and said, "Come Mary, out to the
kitchen and see Tom." I followed Arthur to the kitchen to
see Tom Doill, as I had in a way always liked him, a dark-
haired, rosy cheek boy. But when we reached the kitchen,
there stood a tall, blue-eyed man, although he was Tom, as
they called him, but not Tom Doill. I said "how-da" and
went back to the sitten room till time to get the supper. I
seemed to be all and all with the children, and now they are
all gone—father, mother, Anna, Arthur and Lena.

Well, the Tom of the kitchen proved to be a Thomas
Salmon Moses, Sylvester James' hired man, and I was the

hired girl. So under the circumstances we gradually became acquainted. He found me a good cook, and I found him of a good family, very temperate and thrifty. In those days we didn't look for a man with money, but for a good family, good reputation—many of the boys were chicken thieves. . . . Some women like a man because he is rich, but that kind of like is not lasting, just lasts as long as the pocketbook.

Thomas had always been on a farm. He just loved to work. He was handy, he could do almost anything. In time we became friends, I grew to like him, he was a wonderful man, much better than I am, he was a Christian, always trying to do good to his fellow men. Then as time rolled on, we became engaged. He said he would never leave me, and I don't think he ever has. He is ever with me, even right now.

I believed, when we started out, that we were a team and I had to do as much as my husband did, not like some girls, they sit down, and then somebody has to throw sugar at them. I was always striving to do my share.

My Wedding

On September 20, 1887 Thomas Salmon Moses and Anna Mary Robertson decided to get married. Thomas, as I always called him, had said when he got ready to do for himself, he was a'going to a warmer climate, so we decided to go South. Thomas knew a Mr. Tibbits who had a horse ranch in North Carolina, so Thomas went to see him. Mr. Tibbits was only too glad to get him to go and take charge of the ranch. Then it was decided that we leave about the first of November. "Those that know nothing, fear nothing."

My wedding was kind of unexpected. The Sunday before I introduced Thomas to my parents, and then, Friday, the fourth day of November, Thomas came and brought a large packing box for me to put in my clothing, books and bedding, feather ticks and pillows and so forth. He would take it to his father's and when we got located, they would ship it down to us with some things he had.

On the morning of the 9th of November I bid mother and father good-bye for the time, not knowing when I would see them again. Father felt bad when I came away, he realized I might be going for a long time, like his sisters and brothers. They only got as far as Buffalo, but it was as hard to get to Buffalo as it is to go to Europe today. Father liked Thomas very much, he was all right, couldn't have been better in his way of thinking.

❖

My sister Sarah came to me with my flowers. That was a surprise to me. They were yellow chrysanthemums. She had brought them in before the frost and kept them in the cellar, unknown to everyone, she had saved them. "I know they are not the right kind," she said, but that was all she had. Yellow was supposed to cause jealousy, that's why they were not the right color. I gave the flowers to Thomas' grandmother, she kept those for the longest time.

Brother Joseph drove me to the train, for which I gave him a silver dollar, which he kept as long as he lived. He said it was his lucky penny. At Eagle Bridge I took the train to Hoosick Falls, there I met his sister, Maria, a Mrs. Peters, and there I would meet him, Thomas. Then we were to drive to his home in Hoosick Falls, where all of his sisters would meet me, and we were to have a dinner and meet more of Thomas' people, his grandmother, a Mrs. Whitehead from England, who had spent forty years on each side of the Atlantic, and an aunt, a Mrs. Wilder, one of what they called, "a big shot of Hoosick Falls." She was a very nice lady.

After dinner, Thomas' brother Walter drove the buggy down to the minister, and we went in to be married in the front room. In those days they didn't do so much, and it was no real wedding, but that was quite customary to go off and get married.

Mattie Moses and Charlie Prebble were engaged, they stood up with us. We were married at five o'clock, just as the sun was going down.

Thomas was dressed in black. And I was dressed in a going-away costume of a very dark green dress, and jacket the same, a hat, the same, trimmed with a pink feather. The first thing I had on was a chemise, then my corsets, a corset waist, a pair of pantsies, a little flannel skirt, the bustle, a white skirt, then the dress. The dress was made with a skirt lining and wigging stitched on up to the knees, and the dress cloth went over that, a long skirt reaching to the floor. Then an over-skirt over that, that reached the floor and was tucked up on the sides and the top. Long stockings, black, and high-buttoned shoes. That time they commenced to wear jersey knit jackets, very heavy, the lining and the cloth was all one. I didn't need a coat with all the skirts I had on. Then I had a stiff high collar and white linen cuffs. My dress was all braided in the front, and the long jacket I wore, that was also braided. We bought the braid in patterns. My gloves were tan-colored, doe skin, they called them. And then, the ring.

I never cared for a ring, I never thought anything about those things. I never cared so much for jewelry in those days. I think a good deal more of them now than I did then, maybe it's because I see more of it.

Didn't have a handbag, only a money purse, which I carried in the pocket of my green jacket. Then Thomas carried the rest, I only had $30. His sister had made him a bag. She had taken a red cloth and she worked on it with a short and long stitch; in that he carried his money, inside his undershirt; he just took out enough for the day. But we didn't have so much, I think we only had $600 in cash when we went down there, both together. It went farther than it would today.

The Domini's wife had a wedding cake and table all ready for us, but we could not wait. I saw it and it was very pretty. I just could thank her—and then away. We had to hurry over to take the six o'clock train going to New York City. As luck would have it, it was an excursion train, and all the neighbors were on it, that was a giveaway. They'd all come and congratulate us, and they scolded him for taking away the best girl in the country.

But Mattie and Charlie went back and ate our wedding supper.

Going South

That was a beautiful day, cold and clear. We left the train in Albany to spend the night with my aunt Sophia who had come back from Chicago. She was a dress maker. She

[57]

had a little coal cook stove in her kitchen—you could pick it up and carry it somewhere—and she baked a cake in there and called that my wedding cake, and we had that for supper; she had the other fixings with it, hot biscuits and so on.

They say, if the day you are married is bright and pretty, you are going to lead a bright life, but if it is stormy, you are going to lead a stormy life. The day of the wedding is the bride's day, the following day is the bridegroom's day. My day was bright, and the next day was stormy. Well it's just a saying, I don't think there is anything in it. They also say, "Happy is the bride that the rain falls on" and "Happy is the bride that the snow falls on." I have led a very happy life. Of course, I had trouble, but I kind of brushed it off, I tried to teach myself to forget it, and that everything is going to come off in the end anyway.

The next day at three o'clock we left to take the train for New York, getting in—it rained all the way down— in the evening, and wanted to take the train for Washington. There we were told we would have to cross over to Jersey City to get a train for Washington, and we had just an hour to get there. So we asked the way and started. Walk so many blocks, then take the trolley, then walk a block, then take the elevated railway and go to such a street, then walk to the street cars, the street cars were driven by mules and horses in those days, go so far, then take the ferry. When we got in front of the ferry, they were lifting up the gangplank and somebody see us coming and motioned to us to hurry. My husband took the two suitcases and I gathered up my skirts high—they could see the top of my shoes anyway—and heeled it, I struck the

[58]

gangplank with one foot and landed on the other side, right into the ferry. I glanced around, and there were three men, and I thought, that isn't the room for me, and I went right through to the next door, and I just stopped in time from landing out in the Hudson. The boats were small in those days, when I think back at them. Our trunks had to go eight miles around the city by mule. But we made it. Then we were on our way to Washington.

We reached there 6 o'clock next morning and took a cab to the hotel. Not knowing Washington, or anything about the hotels, we landed at the Virginia Hotel, a very old hotel and not very convenient. We stayed there till about noon, and then we took a train for Staunton, Virginia.

But we had taken the wrong car, and they switched us off to Strasburg. We reached there just at dark, so we had to stay there overnight. It's a beautiful little country village, but it was a kind of an offshoot from the main railway. That night there was the greatest lot of hunters coming in, to go up into the Alleghenies to hunt deer. So the house wasn't quiet all night long, but slam bang, slam bang. And the landlady had her house filled up with those boarders that had come and brought their wives and their children, and we had to take her room, it was next to the hall, and it was a very noisy night. Very little sleep for that time.

Then in the next afternoon about 2 o'clock we took the train for Staunton, Virginia, it was a lovely trip. We reached Staunton about sundown. It was beautiful in the Shenandoah Valley there. We left the ground all frozen up North, and the flowers were in bloom down there.

I was tired and said, "Let us stay here over Sunday," and Thomas was willing, so we started for the Old Virginia

[59]

Hotel, but as soon as I saw it, I did not want to go there, a three-story black brick building and pigs running around the yard. So I said, "Let's find a private boarding place," so we went on up the street and met a boy coming down. We stopped him and asked him for a boarding place, and he said, "Yes Mam, right over there," pointing to the East "and up there," pointing back. We looked at the first house, it was nice and new, but the upper house looked old and antique. The windows hung out over the street. So we went there, the steps lead up the side of the house to a very fancy front door. Thomas rapped on the old beautiful knocker. A lady came to the door and Thomas said, "I am a Mr. Moses from New York State and this is my wife and we would like to get board for over Sunday." It was the first time I heard him call me his wife. And she said, "Come in and welcome." We went into a large hall and then into a sitting room where there were several ladies. The house belonged to a widow woman by the name of Bell and her five children. She was trying to make a living for herself and her children and keep them in school, nice old South-erner. After a time we had supper; my husband got to talk-ing with one of the ladies and he told her we were on our way to North Carolina, and she threw up her hands and said, "Oh no, you must not go there!" Then the others said, "Oh no, there is nothing there but niggers and fleas."

After supper my husband went down to a drug store for some shaving soap, and as soon as he stepped in the store Mr. Bell says to him, "You don't belong here." My hus-band said, "Why not?" "Oh you roll your R's." Mr. Bell was our landlady's cousin, but we did not know it then. Well, Thomas and Mr. Bell got to talking and Bell wanted to know who he was and where he was going and what he was a'going to do and Thomas told him all he thought he had ought to know. And Mr. Bell told him above all things not to go any farther south, that this, the Shenandoah Valley, was the paradise of the world, and so they talked till late. We thought he had got lost and Mrs. Bell got worried and sent her son to the cousins to see if Mr. Moses was there. Well, Mr. Bell had about persuaded Thomas not to go any farther. He said he wanted to help him and said, "Now you come down tomorrow evening and I'll drive you out to a little farm that my brother is on. He doesn't like the land and wants to get into something else."

So Thomas waited around all the next day, Sunday, for evening, though he thought this is a funny time to look at a farm. When they commenced to light up the lamps, he went down to the drug store, as Mr. Bell had asked him to. But as soon as he entered the store, Mr. Bell said, "I told you to come down this evening," and Thomas said, "this is evening." Mr. Bell looked at him and laughed, "Oh, you people call it afternoon, we call it evening after 12 o'clock in the day! It's too late to go out tonight, come down in the morning, and we'll go out. I know you will like it, and you try it for a year, Tom, before you settle down." He was a friend.

So the next morning Thomas went out to see the little farm of a hundred acres or so, it was a pretty little place, and people that were on it did not like to till the soil. They were teachers, and they wished to go back to West Virginia. We could have everything just as they left it.

Then I said, "But Thomas, what about the horse ranch? Are you doing right to back down on that?" And Thomas

[61]

said there had never been no real bargain, he was to go and see if he would like it.

So we agreed to take the little farm, and we moved in that week, taking all of their household supplies, their livestock, even to the chickens and cat. So within thirty days from our marriage we were in a strange land in our own home. Now we were in the swim—it was paddle or sink!

The Bell Farm

We had all the wants of life and good neighbors. I had bought their cow for $25 and twelve old hens for $6, most of their dishes, but I had to have a new stove, and some plates and a coffee mill, some milkpans, a molding board, and I wanted some breadpans, but could not find them. So I had six made at the tin smith's, and they lasted me forty years. I had told my husband that I could not make bread without a molding board, so one day I saw him coming over the hill with it on top of his head. He had ordered it made. The coffee mill was, I think, our first purchase, and now it is quite a curiosity.

Soon my husband bought himself a span of horses and another cow, for which he paid $27. So we each had a cow.

We got our dry-goods boxes from upstate, so we had plenty of bedding and linen and Thomas got his harness and carpenter tools, so he made himself a harrow to have ready for the spring work. But he had a time trying to drive his horses, they didn't understand his language. They were used to "gee haw" and so forth.

I made a box so that I could sow some seeds for early plants; then it commenced to rain, and it did rain! Evergreens all blossomed out with what looked like orchids. They were beautiful. But while it was raining with us, back up North it was snowing, that was when they had the blizzard in New York State in 1888. We did not feel it.

Then Thomas went down to Staunton and bought 40 bushels of potato seed to have ready for planting. Times moved on swiftly, two of my old hens commenced to set, so I sent three dozen eggs down the road and exchanged them for brown leghorn eggs, to put under my setting hens. They did fine. I continued all the rest of the spring till I had 118 little chicks from my 12 old hens. They are lots of care but good company. In the morning I would tie the old hen to a brick and put her and her brood out in the sun. If a shower came up, very little trouble to bring into the woodshed brick, hen and brood.

Then we commenced to have plenty of milk and I commenced to make butter. Our neighbor, Mrs. Carter, wanted to know what we were a'going to do with so much butter. I told her I would trade it out at the store. I'd never get rich that way, she said. You could buy all the butter you could carry for 8 cents a pound. (But you could not eat it.) Mrs. Carter was one good woman, so kind and thoughtful. She would never come over to see me without bringing us a gallon jar of cherry or apple butter. She knew we did not have it, so kept us well supplied. I hope she has her reward.

Well along in May, I had some nice churnings so I asked Thomas to take it down to a grocery store and trade it out for groceries. It was a hot morning, and I was afraid the butter would get warm, so I wrapped it in my best linen napkins—had put it up in 3-pound rolls—then into new tin milk pans, wrapping all with burdock leaves to keep it cool.

[63]

Thomas took it in to a Mr. Spitlar and asked if he could trade it out, and Mr. Spitlar took his jack knife out of his pocket and tasted the butter and said yes, he was getting plenty of butter but would allow me twelve cents in trade. So Thomas took it in sugar as he knew I would want plenty of that as berries commenced to ripen. Mr. Spitlar took the butter home with him, as he said he wanted his people to see some Yankee butter. In a few days after that he sent us word to bring all the butter that we had to spare, and he would give us 15 cents a pound for it. Then when we sent in the next lot he said, "I'll give you 20 cents a pound for all of your butter this summer." So that was settled and by October 20th, I had sold butter enough to pay for our two cows.

Up till then we had spent very little money as we lived on what we had. One day Mrs. Carter told me she had delicious sweet cherries, but they had worms in them. I was afraid to can them, but she told me to pick them and put them in the back of the stove, where it was warm, and the worms would all crawl out. I took her advice and put up sixty-two quarts of cherries and as much more of dewberries. Then there were peaches and pears and lots of other fruit. It was the first time in my life that I had seen so much fruit, and I made the best of it.

That summer Mr. Eakle, Mr. Spitlar's brother in law, came to see us. He wanted us to go down the river onto a 600 acre farm that he had, near Fort Defiance. It was a dairy farm and he wanted us to make butter for him, he had a good market for it. At first Thomas said no, then Mr. Eakle came again and said "I'll grant you 50 cents a pound for every pound you can furnish for a year." Then Thomas said, if he could get his sister to come down there he would try it. Not long after that, Mattie wrote that she and Charlie were to be married in October and wanted to come South. That pleased Thomas, as he thought that I should not be working so hard and Mattie would be so much help to me.

Then one day Thomas had to go down to the Eakle place to complete their bargain. He knew he would be gone all day, so he got a colored boy to come to feed the pigs and milk cows, which he did, till it came to milking my cow. She was a pretty thing, but high-headed, and the colored boy was afraid of her. So I had to go out and milk her. My, but my hands and arms were lame the next day!

The 15th of October Charlie and Mattie came, and so delighted. We had a fine time and everything was so new to them. Mrs. Carter knew they were coming, so the next morning while we were all at the breakfast table, here came Mrs. Carter. She walked right in with an old Plymouth hen under one arm and a game rooster under the other arm and placing them on Mattie's and Charlie's knees, "There is my wedden present from an old rebel." It was their first introduction to the South. They did not know what to say or how to thank her. She was one good woman, but oh so rough and uncouth. But she was a friend indeed.

❖

Well things passed off swiftly and pleasant. We had to get ready for the big farm and there was a'plenty to do, packing up my cans of fruit so as to send them down on a lumber wagon. I thought the best way was to pack it in boxes of wheat wrapped in paper, which I did, and it went through safe.

The Dairy Farm

On November 20th 1888, we left the Bell Farm to go farther down the river to the dairy farm near Fort Defiance which we had rented from Mr. Ed Eakle, buying out all the stock and machinery. Charlie and Mattie were going with us. It was 15 miles down to that farm so we baked bread, pies, cake and meat to take with us the day before, so as to have something to eat when we got there into an empty house.

That day we got up at 3 o'clock in the morning to get our breakfast and take down the stove and beds and pack all on two lumber wagons. The cows, we had but two of them, were to be driven, the pigs and chickens had been taken the day before. I had half a barrel of flour, so I tucked a table cloth down on it, then I packed all of my tin ware on top of the flour, so as to fill the barrel, tying a cloth over the barrel to protect its contents. That was placed in the back of Charlie's wagon. Then in my nice new wash boiler I packed some of our food. In the wash tubs I packed some more with the bread and table dishes. Well, they made out to get it all on the wagons.

Then about 7 o'clock, here comes a colored boy with a splendid team of horses and a double carriage. That was to carry the ladies down to their new home. We soon left, as it was a long drive, and it was a hot day.

But that was Election Day down there, and Charlie and Thomas had to stop and cast their votes as they passed through Staunton. They had gone about five miles when the cows got off the road, down into a deep brook, and the farther they swam the steeper the banks grew. Charlie could not get them out. He thought they would be drowned. He left his horses, they backed and upset his load of furniture. But nothing was broken, only the flour barrel went upside down, and the rolling pin banged into my nice new pie tins, marking them for life. But they lasted for twenty years after that. Well, the boys got the cows out of the creek and loaded the wagon again and started on.

Meanwhile we ladies were travelling on down the river with no care or worry, reaching our new home about 3 o'clock in the afternoon. Our colored boy let us out to a new house with no keys and no one around. The boy then went on home. But we expected Thomas and Charlie to be along soon, so we waited, and we waited, saw the neighbors come out after their dinners and go to work in the fields, and still no Thomas or Charlie. We were tired and hungry. There was a black walnut grove below the house, so we went down there and cracked some and ate them. But that did not satisfy. Mattie was still hungry and said, "Where is the load of garden truck that the boys brought down yesterday?" I said I thought it was put up in the barns, so away we hiked up to the barns. There we found the produce, but how could we eat without cooking, we had no fire or dishes! Mattie said, "I can eat raw cabbage." But we had no knife to cut it with. We banged it against a rock, so we could eat some of it. But that did not satisfy. There were fine beets, but no way to cook them; there were onions, but Mattie said, "How can we eat those without salt and bread?" So we gave that up as a bad job and came back down to the house.

It was getting cold and would soon be dark. Then we saw a man going by the house, and Mattie asked him if he would break open the door, so that we could get into the house. He hated to do that, but after a time he got a window opened and Mattie crawled through and opened a door that was bolted. Then she asked him for some matches, which he happened to have. He was a Mr. Alexander, was to be one of our neighbors, a good friend.

Well, we got into the house and built a fine chip fire in the parlor fireplace, so we had some light and warmth when the boys got there. We could hear them coming acrost the ford in the river. They had a time getting the cows acrost. They had seen enough of water for one day. Then the boys hurried up the lane to see how we had made out through the day. They were worried nearly sick, but when they found us all right, then there was rejoicing. Mr. Ed Eakle had followed them down from Staunton, so he was some help with the cows at the ford, and when they got to the house, he helped them to unload, set up the stove, fill and light the lamps, so we could have lights, bring in the table and chairs and food.

As soon as they got a fire in the stove and had hot water for coffee, I had creamed up a lot of cold potatoes. Mattie had got the table set, then we all sat down to a good supper with bread, butter and pickles, slices of beef, cold beans, catsup, apple pie and so forth. We talked and planned and told all the troubles we had seen through the day.

Then Mr. Eakle went over to his brother's to sleep that

night. While Mattie and I were doing up the dishes, the boys were setting up the beds for the time being.

The next day we tried to make the house cosy and comfortable. Mattie took the room acrost the large hall, and I took the sitting room for my sleeping room. The boys, as we called Thomas and Charlie, got a little wood stove for my room, so that we had things very comfortable for the time. We had put the cook stove in what was the dining room for the winter, as the kitchen needed renovation.

Those were the days of white-washed walls and sanded floors, sweet and clean. The rooms were very large, twelve feet high and took forty yards of carpet. I needed an extra table, so I had our dry-goods box brought and used it as a table and cupboard.

We had a lovely dairy room with running water on one side of the porch. The porches were on three sides of the house, with glass doors opening on them.

There was plenty of work to do. Soon the milk commenced to come to the house, and that was my work to take care of. Mattie took care of the cooking. So we were doing fine.

Then we sent up into Vermont for a butter print. It had no design on it, so my husband thought he could carve one on it, which he did. Thereafter there was the name of "Moses" in raised letters on every print of butter. It took 20 prints to a tray, there was four trays to a crate, and we wanted to ship out two crates a week. I had only a small churn that we stood on a table, or my dry-goods box, so I would have to churn three and four times a day. We shipped the butter to the White Sulphur Springs in West Virginia.

[69]

Churning three times a day was too tedious, so we sent back North for a barrel churn, then while it was heavy work, it was a pleasure. I could look off down the valley many miles, when trains came through, it was beautiful to watch the smoke rolling out against the Blue Ridge Mountains. How I wished that I could paint a picture of it, the white and grey against the blue!

❖

One day I was very busy, and Mattie was ransacking in the attic and found a very large pair of ladies' hoop skirts and thought what fun it would be to dress up in it. So she did, putting one of my Mother Hubbards on. Then she came where I was, laughing at herself. She could hardly get through the door. Then she heard the front door bell ring and, thinking it was one of the boys, away she went to open the door. I was not presentable, so poor Mattie had to face the company, hoop skirt and all. It was not the boys that time, it was the minister and his wife and another lady. Well, they all made the best of it, but never forgotten.

Winona

December 1st came and I was not much good. Thomas had gone up to the manganese mines and had spoken to Dr. Arbuckle, the doctor there. He said he would come when needed. December 1st I did not leave my room. Sunday, December 2nd, very cold for those parts, Charlie went for Dr. Arbuckle at noon. He was not much good. The baby arrived at 8 o'clock that night. I heard the doctor say it was a girl, the nicest and prettiest baby he ever saw, but maybe that was just all for my good. Mrs. Ray came and dressed the baby for us a few days. Then we got along all right. We named the baby Winona Robertson Moses. I went out to the kitchen and showed them how to make butter prints on the ninth day.

Little Ona was a good child and did not give us any trouble. Those were busy days, sometimes we would have to churn and print up the butter at night, always get up at one o'clock to gather the vegetable and load up the truck wagon so as to leave by four in the morning to be in Staunton by seven o'clock. We would take a load every other day for six months. Hard work, but it paid as far as money is concerned.

Once Thomas went off by the tenant house, and saw this dogwood tree all in bloom. He brought in a branch, it was like half a tree, the whole branch was all in blossom and he put it in the jar of water by one side of the room, and put up a couple of nails to the branches to hold them up, it reached clear to the ceiling. It filled the whole side of the dining room and lasted about a month. It was gorgeous you could hardly believe it, I had never seen anything like that, have never seen it since either.

In the summer of 1889, when baby Moses could sit alone, I would bring her out on the porch, spread a little quilt thereon and set her on it, so she could watch the cats and birds. The cats seemed to like her and would rub up against her. As she got older, she would grab hold of their tails and be dragged off the porch. Then I would have to get up a crying and bruised baby, and nurse her for a while. I soon tired of that and could not get rid of the cats, they were large pretty cats. One day my husband put them in a sack and loaded it on the garden truck, intending to turn them loose when he got acrost the ford, but he had crossed the second ford before he thought of the cats. Then two weeks passed, I missed them, it seemed lonely without them. One gets attached to such things. Then one morning early, I went on the porch and there was Kitty Snooks all wet, Tiger had gone up to the barns, looking for milk I suppose; they had found their way back 15 miles and swam two rivers. It did not seem possible, but must have been. Then I made a jumper for little baby Moses, a little chair out of bed ticking that would just fit, then the straps to carry to the ceiling where I had a strong spring. Now she was up and away from the cats.

As summer advanced the work grew harder in-doors and out. After harvest we had to have thrashers for oats, rye and wheat, wheat principally. There a gang of about six men would go from farm to farm, as they were needed, with a threshing machine. Then we would have to furnish as many more men and the neighbors would furnish two or three wagons, but as a general thing, part of them would be colored men, so we would always have to set two tables. This summer I only had a few hours to get ready for them, and as we were 15 miles from a store where we could get dishes, and I did not know the neighbors, we had to make out with what we had. On a milk pan we had baked beans, boiled ham, sliced, on a board that Charlie had made; on another board we had sliced bread and butter, a pan of mashed potatoes; on six of the dinner plates we placed the berry pies, we gave them milk, buttermilk and water in a pail with a dipper. This was the kitchen for the colored help. They had boxes and stools to sit on. In the dining room they had the same, only they had plates, knives and forks, while I could only give the colored folks butcher knives and pot lids for plates. But no one went hungry.

Apple Butter Making

Late summer was the time for applebutter making. The applebutter was considered a necessity. Early in the season we would make cherry butter, we would make it up by the gallon, those stone gallon jars—I have one left.

To make applebutter, you take two barrels of sweet cider (you grind apples and make sweet cider first), then you put them on in a big brass kettle over a fire out in the orchard and start it to boiling. You want three barrels of quartered apples, or snits, as they called them, with cores taken out, and then you commence to feed those in, and stirring and keeping that stirrer going. The stirrer was a very long stick which would rest on the kettle, with a smaller stick that was held in by a peg going to the bottom of the kettle. Women folks would keep that going, feeding in all the apples till evening. Then the young folks would come in to start stirring. They'd have two—a boy and a girl—to take hold of the handle. They'd have a regular frolic all night out in the orchard. If they'd get this started early enough in the morning, they'd have to stir till about midnight, when it would get thick enough. Then you pour in—if you want it sweet and pleasant—maybe 20 pounds of sugar, and then you put in either cinnamon or clove oil, whatever you like best, and keep tasting it till you have got the right sourness or sweetness and the right flavor. About that time you bring out your jars, around the fire that has gone down, not too hot. We would make about 40 gallons at a time. It was very much like a jelly conserve.

❖

The winter of 1889 we would try to take the butter to town every week, but sometimes the snow would be too deep and then a crust would form on the snow and it would be dangerous to try to drive horses through it. Then the neighbors would bring out their mules and all hands would drive or ride the mules over the roads to break the snow crust. We had two mules, and their legs were small so that the crust did not cut them. Down South I'd seen the deepest snow I had seen in my life. It would come down in big flakes, but didn't last long, about three days.

❖

The Thanksgiving of 1891, Thomas' brother Walter and his wife Zoe came down to visit us, we met them at the train. It was a warm day, we had both doors and windows opened; in Virginia we did not have snow at that time of the year, it was a change from the North where we travelled in sleighs to wherever we were going to Thanksgiving dinner. I was to have a Thanksgiving dinner for them, we had roast turkey with all the trimmens. After dinner we went for a walk down by the river, where there were lots of black walnut trees and we gathered bushels of nuts.

Aunt Carrie

When Loyd was born, on December 2, 1891—three years to the day after Winona—I had a colored mammy come in, and she did for me. We had no doctors. That old colored lady was no good, I found out afterwards, and she was no help to me, I had to kind of take care of myself. But when my other children were born, I got the other nurse, Aunt Carrie, she took charge of everything. All I had to do was to give her $10. She stayed two weeks and did all the washing, ironing and took care of the other children too. She was a wonderful woman.

When she was a little girl, she was raised as a slave, and she was freed before she was very old, and then this old doctor was her master, and his wife. When their oldest daughter was married, Carrie was about ten years old and was given to the daughter to be her maid. Her husband was a Northerner. They had no use for the slaves, only for the work they could get out of them. He whipped her one day, which cut up her back. She still carried the marks. She crawled away and went to sleep. It happened that her old Missis came that day and wanted to know where Carrie was. So someone went to find Carrie, and they got her out. They had to put water on her back to remove the chemise. And the old Missis took her home with her. She would not let them have her any more. And then the old doctor got to taking her with him to help him with his work, and whatever he got to do. He would get so he wouldn't go without her. And there she learned to become quite a nurse, quite a doctor herself, and she could save some of the patients, she said, when he would lose them.

The old doctor died, and Carrie could be called upon in case of illness. She was just a young girl, but everybody knew Aunt Carrie. She was in her thirties when she used to come to me. She was married and had two children.

In our home father always did all the doctoring, with roots and herbs, and I never saw a doctor till I was almost twenty years old.

❖

When Loyd was nine months old, I gave him the clock to play with one day. I hardly got out to the kitchen, I heard him crying, so I came back, and there Winona sat—she hadn't heard me coming—just plucking the hair out of his head. "Ona, what are you doing?" "I want to kill him!" She was jealous of him. His father made a good deal of him, that had something to do with it. She didn't see why he had to be there at all.

❖

I fought long against the Southern accent, and I didn't mingle. I declared that I would never say "bucket" or "tote," but I gradually drifted into it. I got awfully mixed up one day. A little girl had come to visit, and I asked her whether she wouldn't want to take some grapes home to her mother. She asked me if I would give her a poke to carry them in. I didn't know what a poke was, I knew a poke that they put on geese to keep them from crawling

through the fences and on cows to keep them from jump-
ing fences, but I never heard of any other kind of poke.
The poke that she wanted was a paper sack or bag; those
were pokes in the South, they didn't know what a bag was.

The Dudley Place and the Dead Man

Mr. Eakle died and the farm had to be sold. So we moved
to another farm nearer Staunton. There was no convenience
of butter making in the new place, which was just a common farm, the Dudley place.

So we commenced to sell milk. My husband peddled milk
in bottles. The milk was milked and strained, and then I
used to bottle it and seal the bottles with paper and put
them in boxes, about twenty bottles in a box. We had to
have from six to more men, as the milking had to be done
by hand. Thomas had a two-horse produce wagon and de-
livered the milk and the cream wherever it was ordered, but
no more butter making. My husband had peddled milk in
Hoosick Falls, so it was nothing new for him. For me it was
less work, although I had from sixty to a hundred milk
bottles to wash every day, but not so much cooking to do,
only by times. And as this was an old brick house, three
stories high, I gave up the lower rooms and therefore had
to carry wood and water up seventeen steps to the kitchen.
Hard work, but it was very nice.

After we took the Dudley place, we hired a colored
man. When he was a little boy, he was Andy Baily, and
then when he left Baily, he went with this Mr. Stewart, and
then he was Andy Stewart. He was freed when he was
about three years old, but he still would take on the mas-

ter's name, because he didn't have any of his own. The nine years he lived with us he was Andy Moses. That was so if he had any letters come or anything, they could find him.

He helped with all the farm work, plowing and haying or things like that he did, very faithful. He was just like one of our own, but he'd never come to the table with us. He never had, and he didn't think it was his place; it was customary there that the colored people all eat in the kitchen. But if we got sick, we had the grippe twice, he'd nurse us, make our coffee, tea, toast, if we wanted. He lived right with us, had his room, had all his property, his horse and buggy there. And weekdays, he'd go out and take the kids with him. Sundays he would go out driving. In those days children had lots of clothes on, even in summer, but he'd take them by the barn and pull the pantsies off the babies, so they'd get some air on them. He was just as much interested as though they were his own kids.

One day Charlie and Thomas sat down in the kitchen talking, and we got tired and kind of half-way started for bed, and Andy had not got home yet, and we went to the door—it was a beautiful, moonlight night—and Mattie says—she was leaning over the porch in the back kitchen —"Do you see that wagon coming? That's Andy." "Yes," I said, "I wouldn't be surprised if that was Andy." And she says, "Oh, I just would love to scare the blue beans out of him." "All right, what will we do?" "Oh, I know, let's make up a scarecrow to put up in the wagon shed." "All right."

So we ran down to the wash room underneath, there was a lot of dirty clothes on the basin, waiting for next morning to be washed, such as table cloths, sheets and overalls

[78]

and shirts. We stuffed the overalls full with the soiled clothes, then we stuffed the shirt, then tacked them together, stuffed a pillow slip to make a head, tacked it on to the shirt, and ran right down with it to the wagon shed, carrying a sheet and a table cloth. Up over the wagon shed was a big wheel. She climbed up on that and dragged the sheet over, so it would flap when the door was opened, with the breeze. Then we hung the man underneath it and hitched it to the post of the door. Oh, we had it all planned. Poor Andy! After we had it done, we heeled it back, because we could hear the horse and buggy coming. We went underneath the brick work and stood there and listened for Andy. We could hear him singing to himself till he got to the wagon shed. Then all was quiet. He unhitched his horse and put it in the stable, then he went back to push his buggy into the shed. As he opened the door, the post that the door was hitched to dropped, and down came the dead man, and the dead man hopped right at him, he said, it jumped right up at him. We heard him coming towards the house, and we heeled it towards our rooms. Mattie went into her room and stuffed the pillow case into her mouth, and I buried my face in the pillow, in my room. We had hardly got settled till we heard Andy come to his room. "Oh, Mr. Moses, oh, Mr. Moses, come here quick, there is a dead man!" Thomas and Charlie started to come and see what the trouble was. And then Thomas thought and called: "You girls been up to anything?" No, we were sound asleep. "Come now, Mr. Moses!" So, they went trotting down the back stairs, down to see the dead man, and going down, he told them all about it. Thomas thought

[79]

there was a rat somewhere, he didn't know where, but the minute he saw it, he knew.

Andy didn't look or speak to us the next day. Mattie told him, "Well, you mustn't be out so late at night." It was 10 o'clock then.

The Old Captain

They always laugh about me, but I think I saw a spirit at the Dudley place; I don't know if it was so, but I think so anyway. We had upstairs what I used for a dining room, and the room over the kitchen downstairs I had for a kitchen upstairs. Then there was a long flight of stairs going up to the chambers. There we had three large sleeping rooms, and I had the largest one for myself, I had two beds in it.

Loyd was about a year old, I used to have him take his nap about four o'clock. That evening I had taken Loyd up to take his nap, I had lain him down on the bed and lain down with him myself, thought I would stay there until Thomas came in. I didn't drop off to sleep, but I was there, very quiet, with my eyes closed. All at once I looked out in the room, and there stood a man, and he stood right where I had a little round table, and as I looked at him, the table seemed to be a square stand and a big book on it, and he was turning the pages of the big book. He was quite an old man, his hair was grey, something like father used to wear it, he had on spectacles, a black frock coat. His nose was long and was humped in towards his lip. And I said, "How did you come in here, where did you get that book, and where are my flowers that were on the table?" I looked him over good, I could almost draw a picture of him now. He was standing there, where the stove should be, and pretty soon I heard something downstairs, and he commenced to fade, and I expect it was Thomas coming, and when Thomas came into the room, my man had all vanished, and Thomas stood near the table, and I couldn't believe it, and I said to Thomas, "I have seen a ghost!" And he says, "Oh, you had been dreaming," and I said, "No, I had not been dreaming, I had not shut my eyes." But my ghost was gone, and I described it to Thomas, and he laughed at me till the next day, when our neighbor Mr. Keister, came in, and they told him about it, and Keister said: "That was the old captain that had built this house, he must have come back for some of the evil deeds he did." For a long time I could not get it out of my mind, but then it vanished. I never believed in those things, but it was like a vision.

❖

The Dudley place was Forrest's birthplace. When he was little, I thought if I had a cradle, if I would mend and had the cradle going, it would be a good thing to have. Our hired girl, a Mrs. Saenger, she was a "grass widow," they called her; she didn't live with her husband. She knew one of the neighbors had two cradles, and she thought I could get one of them. He was a cabinet maker and had made them for his children. One day, after the dinner was over and the dishes done up, she had the colored man hitch up the horse, called "Old Bogus," to the buggy and she took Ona, Loyd and her little girl, same age as Loyd, and she

[81]

started over to Mr. Fauver, they were friends of hers in a way. They had to ford the river, we had no bridges. Andy and she had had a little discussion at the table at dinner time. They started out, it was all down hill until they got to the river. She claimed he didn't hitch the tracers onto the wagon, he just left them loose, and when she got into the river, the horse walked right out of the shafts, but she had hold of the reins, but what could she do? There she had two babies and Ona by the side of her in the middle of the river, so she had to sit there and holler for help. There was a man across the river, and after a time Mr. Chandler came to the rescue. He unhitched one of the horses and rode it out into the river and hitched Old Bogus on as it should have been. And she went on acrost the river to her friends and got the little cradle. They took it on the back of the buggy, and she came home, with the intention of "killing that nigger." She thought he had done it on purpose, but I don't think so. The colored people and the poor white people were envious of each other and they were always in a jangle.

❖

About that time Aunt Hattie came down South. Thomas had been home to visit his father who was poorly. She came to get me ready to go home next spring. I had never been back home. She stayed all winter. She brought a lot of this knit red goods from Bennington, she thought it would be nice for the children, and she made little Forrest three little shirts, long sleeves they had in those days, and I don't know how many stockinettes. She was very nice with the needle. Then she'd dress him up in his little red shirt and

[82]

stockings and toss him up with her hand and say: "See my little monkey, see my little monkey, I wished I had a dozen!"

When spring came, I was in no condition to go visiting, so she had to go back without me.

❖

I used to wear in those days Mother Hubbard dresses. Some were gathered back and front, full, like a sack, they made a pretty dress if you belt 'em in. I had what they called a wrapper when Ona was born. It was gored, black festooned, deep lace down the front of it, if you looked at me, you'd see the lace, you didn't see me.

When Forrest and Loyd were along four and five years old, I made a blue cotton star, the "Star of Bethlehem" and set it on Forrest's night dress, so he could tell it from Loyd's nightie. They were a year and a half apart, and they would fight every year, because all at once there was two years' difference between them; they couldn't figure that out.

❖

In the summer I used to put sun bonnets on the children to keep them from getting freckled and tanned, and tie them so they coudn't throw them in the river. There was quite a long foot-bridge, suspended very high above the water. It was for pedestrians to go across, and by the side there was a fording for the horses and carriages. I never was around, and the children got so used to playing on the bridge before I ever knew what they were doing. But when I first went acrost it, I would have given anything to go back when I got right out in the middle of the bridge, but I went on, and afterwards I got so I used to run acrost it. Those children playing on the bridge used to worry me a little bit. Thomas said, "No use worrying."

The time we had the flood, the water ran right over it. The flood was caused from a long rain in the month of June, and all the reservoirs near Staunton broke loose. In the night I heard the calves bleating and I thought they were down on the river flat. I went down the kitchen stairs, by the horse barn, past the shed where we scared Andy, and I could see that the river was above the bridge, but the calves were above in high land. I thought I'd go back and kind of hurried up the road to the house, and just as I got there, a wave struck the barnyard gate, pitch, pitch, but I couldn't see it plain enough, it took the gate right along with it. That wave came clear down from Staunton, 8 or 10 miles, and was caused by one of those burst reservoirs. It came right through the city of Staunton, and I think quite a few people were drowned. They didn't have time to get away.

❖

Then Anna was born, so I had four babies to care for. But we got along very nice till the children got the scarlet fever, that was a hard year but it passed on like all the rest.

❖

I didn't bring up the children, they kind of come up. They were always with me in the house helping, till they started into school, and I believe I got more out of them before

The first picture, painted on the fire board in the parlor

ne of the early worsted pictures, showing Grandma Moses' home in Eagle Bridge

they've gone to school than afterwards, because—it was a big house—they could run on errands a lot. They could run to the chicken house and gather the eggs, and that was women's work there in the South to look after the chickens. When they were little bits of tots, they brought in the wood. We had regular old fashioned toy chairs; they would load the chairs with wood and drag it down to the steps and then carry it up the steps, an armful at a time, till they wore the back legs off the chairs.

❖

In the year of 1896, we went to a fair at Gipsyhill Park, near Staunton, Va. It was a nice country fair, there I entered my first canned fruit, cherries and tomatoes, for which I took first prize. There I took my four children ranging in age from two to eight, but never again! And there I saw my first automobile. It was owned by a Mr. Hausburger. It was as high up as it was long. He would take his wife and child for a ride going from Staunton down the pike to Harper's Ferry on a Sunday afternoon. The next one I saw, a Dr. Waite had. He had come back from the West to his home town and brought the car with him in 1909. But soon they were very plentiful, and now in a way they are a necessity.

❖

Mattie and Charlie were living across the river from us at that time, across the foot bridge. They stayed with us at

[85]

the Eakle place for a few years, then he got a job down at the mill, when the boom of Virginia started, and he went out to Clifton Forge, they had lots of work for him in the mill. They were out there about a year and a half, and he sunk all his money in the boom. They would have a big track of land and divide it up in lots, you would invest your money, and if they sold out quick, you would get a lot, if they didn't, you would get nothing. He got discouraged and tried it on the farm again, on his own hooks. Then he heard his mother was sick and poorly at home, and they came back here. They'd been South eight years. Now Mattie is the only one left of the Moses family,* and I and brother Fred are the only ones left of the Robertson family. So you have to get the younger generation when we are out of the way.

We lived on this farm for eight years. Then Mrs. Dudley was coming back, she was a widow woman. She remodelled the house, her children had come back from school.

Mount Airy

So we bought a farm (all the other places had been rented), called Dangerfield farm, or "Mount Airy," that's where my youngest son Hugh was born. We were there two years, but schools were far away.

There was a little Episcopal chapel near the Dangerfield place, we used to go across the meadow to the chapel. It set over on the pike, that was a built road, built by con-

* She died in June, 1951.

victs, running from Staunton to Harrisburg. I suppose it is a state road yet. It was built by pounding rocks. They'd take the convicts out of the jail, chain gang, they called them, and they pound this rock till it was probably an inch and a half thick or smaller, and the road was kept covered with that for years, and by driving heavy teams over it, it gradually pulverized the rocks. It would be 3 feet deep in places, quite a broad road. You could hardly go to Staunton without seeing a small gang breaking rock. Once I saw one of them breaking away, he run down through our yard, down through Sandy Hollow, and I see the man going, and I says, "Where is he going, what is he running for?" And it wasn't long till some officers came looking for him, they knew just where to look for him. He had got loose off the chain.

We went over to this little chapel, every Sunday they'd have meetings there, and all the women could come and bring their babies, and someone was supposed to take care of them; by the side they had built a little nursery. I took Hugh a few times, but he would squawl, he didn't like to stay. I could hear his voice above all the rest, and then I would have to get out and get him and take him home.

All denominations would come there on communion day, Presbyterians, Baptists, Methodists and Unitarian brothers, all took communion, there was no partiality one way or the other. And that Mr. Jet was minister.

That's where we were all baptized. Thomas had been baptized, but the rest of us hadn't. I did it because I thought it wasn't right not to be all one. We stood by the altar, and the minister just sprinkled us. It didn't make any differ-

[87]

ence with me, didn't change me. It wasn't customary to baptize children, I don't remember ever hearing of anyone being baptized until I was well grown up, only certain people were. Way back in my grandmother's day they must have had baptism, because I heard of her telling me of the dresses the children wore over in the Cambridge church. And up here the Baptists wait till they are big enough to dip them under water six feet down. There was a good many baptized here several years ago right out in the Owl Kill, the minister would dip them in over their heads and say a prayer, and then they'd heel it home to get on dry clothes.

I had not named Hugh at that time. There was one of the Sunday school teachers, and she asked me, "What have you decided to name the baby?" He was then nine months old, he was just called "baby" or "boy" or "kid," as it would come along, same as you would a cat. I says, "I don't know, I haven't really decided." So she says, "Why don't you call him Hugh?" That was her brother's name, Hugh Worthington. "That's a beautiful name," she said. "Well, it's as good as any," I said, so he was baptized Hugh Worthington Moses. At that time I don't think they kept any records of birth, not when Ona was born. We couldn't get it when Ona went to school; they wanted it, but we couldn't get it, and the doctor had died.

❖

We had ten children, but there were only five that grew. One lived to be six weeks, and the others were dead born, still born, they called it. But they had to have graves just the same—five little graves I left in that beautiful Shenandoah Valley.

❖

Then in August of 1903 we got a chance to sell the farm, and we were to come home right away. They had a sale, and we sold nearly everything. But there were some things I would not sell, I would not sell my cow. I told my husband that I could not go North with the children and going to be cold there, they were not dressed for it. He said, "We'll go up to Staunton and take a few rooms, and you can sew up there as much as you please." But when he got to Staunton, he couldn't find a place nor rooms of any description. He hunted all day. Then he got two real estate men to hunt with him, and they could find nothing. You see, Staunton is a city of schools, and the young people were coming from all directions to go to school and trying to find living quarters. Everything was taken up but what they could crawl into.

Mount Nebo

Then they offered him, outside the city limits, a little farm with a very nice house and out-buildings. He was so pleased with it, he came right to me to look at it. I told him it was all satisfactory to me if he liked it, and we would try it. The next week we started moving in, and the people that were there were already moved out. Down at the bank it was very nice, a beautiful place. There was a

[89]

large vineyard on it, but there was not much farm work, only 20 acres. We kept our two cows, so we lived good. One of the two was my old cow. We took in the mail man, Mr. Greer. He lived too far down, so he boarded with me, and he called our place Mount Nebo, that's where Moses disappeared.

We stayed there two years, and the children went to school. My husband had to have something to do, there was not much work, so he agreed to take charge of one of the neighbors' places, at $50 a month, cheap, wasn't it? Part of the time he was there, and part of the time he was home again.

One day I asked him, if I would pay the grocer's bill, if he would give me the money that he pays out every Saturday. "Certainly," he said, "you can have all the money you want." So, that night, when the children went to the sitten room to their studies, I went into the store room and got three potatoes, large ones, pared them and put them in soaking water. Then I went up and joined the rest. But we went to bed early that night. The next morning I slipped downstairs, not letting them know that I was up, and sliced my potatoes just as fine as I could slice them for potato chips. As soon as the children had started for school, I heated up my lard, dragged up my potato chips and got ready to fry, so that they wouldn't know anything about it. Then I fried my chips till I had a pound of them, slightly salted, and put them in a paper "poke." When the children came home for dinner, I sent them down the street to my grocer man and asked him how much he would allow me for a pound of chips in trade. I was a'going to buy my own groceries to save money. He gave me 25 cents in trade. And that night, when Loyd was coming home from school, he called him in and told him he was going to take another two pounds in the morning. I had to get busy, but I sent them down the next noon as they went back to school. Then there came an order for five pounds, I was getting rich! Then he raised on the prices, he gave me 30 cents from then on but kept on increasing the quantities. I had to make 10 pounds a week, and slicing them by hand, that was something. So my husband made a slicer. He didn't have much faith in it, he thought it would soon wear off, it was too laborious, but it increased till I had to make them by the barrel and send them to White Sulphur Springs and over to Charlottesville besides keeping this man furnished with them.

Well, that was the potato chip business. Always wanted to be independent, I couldn't bear the thought of sitting down and Thomas handing out the money—just like climbing the house in my childhood days, I wanted to be the big toad.

Aunt Peachy

Near our place, down what they called Sandy Hollow, there were a dozen or more huts, or shanties, of different families, all colored, and Aunt Peachy, a great, big, fat darkie woman, had the largest one; she lived in the "mansion," they said. She did beautiful washing to make a living, but she never worked for me; she would go downtown to do her washing there. The time of the big flood she was in the "factory" in Staunton. The flood washed tubs and all out of the door. If ever she prayed in her life, she did then, she said. It had been raining so long, she had 4 or 5 tubs full of different washings, waiting for the time to hang them up. They stood on benches in this one room. She went up the stairs, and the flood washed everything down through the valley. She saw she couldn't get out, and she went to her window, trying to get help. Men were going around on horseback, helping people to get out all they could, but she couldn't get out of the window. The man swung his horse to the window, and she prayed to the Lord to help her. He told her to get her feet out. "So I prayed to the Lord and just struck my feet out and I squirmed till I got out on the horse's back," she said. It was as good as a circus to hear her.

When she was young, she was a slave, she always had the plowing to do. At that time the slaves didn't have more than one garment or wrapper, made of heavy cloth, and this day she was plowing and she had on her wrapper, and going under a bush with the plow, she felt something and she thought it was a lizard. She was deathly afraid of lizards, just as afraid as of poisonous snakes, and she knew if this lizard bit her, she knew she would be a "dead nigger"—that's the way she put it. And she was so scared, she threw her wrapper right off and kept on running, calling on God to save her, until she got to her cabin, for a half a mile, maybe. "I was so scared," she said.

This old Aunt Peachy gave the children their first Easter eggs. She told Hugh and Anna on Easter morning that the old bunny would come at night and if they were a-bed and asleep, he would leave the bunnies' eggs on the front porch. Sure enough, when they got up in the morning, there were two baskets filled with candy and some flowers and two big bunny eggs. And the eggs, those china eggs, were large and filled with candies. That gave them more faith what the bunnies would do for Easter. Anna used to keep hers in her work basket to darn the stockings on. That shows that woman's disposition, she hardly knew the children much, still she gave them something. She was a good old soul.

Brownie

Hugh was two or three years old, and he wanted a dog. He had a penny, and he gave it to his father to buy him a dog with. So this night Thomas came home with a little dog in his breast pocket. It was a rainy evening. He came into the dining room, and he knew that Hugh would come to him and climb up on his knee and go through his pockets for candy or string or something like that. And Hugh plunged his hand in and felt this little dog and was scared, and he dropped down off his father's lap and ran across the room to Ona for protection, because there was something in the pocket that didn't feel right. His father took out the little puppy dog and gave it to Ona. We had a light blue bowl that would hold a cup-full, and he put the puppy in that little bowl, and his head was covered, so you can see how small that dog was. Ona had to take care of it for all of the next year. She likes any animals that have four legs. It was a great pet, and we had it for twenty years. His name was Brownie. We still had it

[93]

when my grandson Edward—Hugh's oldest child—was a baby. In the end it went blind.

❖

In the fall of 1905 father and mother came down to visit, and my brother Fred. My brother Lester had come when Ona was a baby and spent the winter, and my sister Ona came down that winter too. Ona liked it well enough, but she got homesick. She was always a lady, and the young people in the South were not her style. So she did not have any associates and she came back here. She was a dress maker by profession. She went to California and stayed there for a good many years.

My husband was back North two or three times, but I didn't care to come. He had planned four or five years that we would go back. He was homesick, and each time he went back he had been more homesick than before.

Going Back North

While father and mother were there, a man from Pennsylvania came down and wanted to get a new home, he thought it would be warmer for his wife and daughter, and he bargained for our place, and we sold the place to him. Mother said that there were two places for sale near Eagle Bridge and that we could have our pick, if we wanted. So we wrote up and had Lester and my husband's brother Walter go up and look at the places, and they liked one of them so much that they bargained for it, but we had to be there in December. Father and mother and

[94]

brother went home, and we commenced to prepare on moving back. That's how we went to come here.

We chartered a railroad car, and we brought the stuff we had—a piano and beds and necessary things up here that way. By taking a car, we could bring a lot of produce, apples, meat—we butchered a hog—a cow, hens, and stock. With the car, if there was livestock in it, we had to have a man to take care of it, so Thomas went with the car, but he smuggled in the two little boys, Forrest and Loyd, besides himself. They swung our bed spring into the car, to make beds for themselves. They had a little kerosene oil stove for warmth. In one corner was the cow tied up with the feed and the fork for the manure. In another corner was the chicken coop and in the other was the produce. The apples made the whole car smell. And the little black and tan dog went with them too. So now, that was a family. The stove was tied in the center, so the jolting of the car would not tip it over. But at one place, where they were switching off, the jolt was so strong, it knocked the cow off her feet, she went down on her knees, and in so doing, tipped the stove. They were afraid it would tip over, but it didn't. In Scranton the car was hung up on the track for nearly a day, and the two boys were almost discovered. The railroad men smelled the apples, they were Johnson apples, hard and very fragrant. Loyd went up to the door to meet them, for fear they would get up too close and see what was in there. They looked around but they didn't come in. He knew that he was coming without a ticket, and he'd made up his mind to tell a story that he was taking care of the cows and chickens. He still loves to tell

[95]

stories now. Meanwhile Thomas found the head man and got his car hitched on.

That was a laughable trip for them. The price of the car was $60, and it brought all our produce all right here to Eagle Bridge, I think that was a pretty cheap trip.

Hugh, Anna and Ona went with me on the train. We should have gone out from Staunton at 12 o'clock, but we didn't leave till 6 o'clock next morning. All the way up to New York, it was a muggy, rainy day. Anna was sleepy, and I had dropped off to sleep too. When I woke up, she had her feet sticking right out of the window! I had my pocket full of cheese and crackers to keep awake, but I always dropped off to sleep again. So once the conductor came around, gave me a big rap and said: "Shut your mouth, shut your mouth!" Hugh was a little thing, he went off to sleep. Ona would not sit with us, she went down the car and sat with some people, flirting. She was 17. We got into New York that night, and we stayed overnight, but I don't know now where. From New York we took the train up to Eagle Bridge, and we came through to Albany, had to stay there overnight, and came here next morning. The snow was on the ground. That was about the 15th of December.

Going up home—it was, of course, new country to all my "rebels"—a man took us up home. Before we got to my parents' house, we passed the place of an old Irishman, Dennis McMann. He was a funny character. He would do anything to get a living. One time, he took a notion that he wanted some cider. He had apples, so he loaded up his little one-horse spring wagon and started for the cider mill. He got to the Cambridge railroad and on the crossing—it is a very blind crossing—just as he started to cross, the engineer didn't blow his whistle in time and struck the hind part of Dennis' wagon. The wagon wasn't smashed, but he spilled all the apples, and poor Dennis got out to gather them up. The conductor stopped to see if he was hurt. So Dennis pitched into him "What are you stopping now for, when you didn't stop before?"

When we went by that morning, I remembered that story, and said to Ona, "This is where Dennis McMann lives, it looks deserted, all the chickens roosting on the window sill and the door sill, and he either left the country or he is dead." And they said, "Poor old man, he is there all alone and crippled." Nothing more was said until the next day when my father told us "You know, they found Dennis McMann dead, they say he was laying dead in the house when you passed."

So we got home, and it was two days before the car came in with the other bunch. The next day we went down here to look the place over, and they unloaded the car and brought the things in.

And as we went along the old places, I said to Ona, "I don't think a bit has changed since we left here, the gates are hanging on one hinge since I went away"—and I had been gone twenty years. They weren't very progressive here.

Eagle Bridge

CHAPTER THREE

E AGLE BRIDGE was the name of a little hamlet, where close by we had our new dairy farm, and here I am yet, but all alone, "all are scattered now, and fled, some are married some are dead. . . ."

Bridges were landmarks in olden times, people in travelling through the land, they would inquire from one bridge to another. They often had covered bridges, well I think the covering was to protect the timbers from snow and rain, so that they would not decay so fast, as it was quite an undertaking to build a bridge across a rapid flowing stream. But now they are swiftly passing away. There was the Hoosick Bridge, in early days called the White House Bridge, the longest bridge in New York State, and now it is no more.

Eagle Bridge got its name from a large eagle that was painted on one end of the bridge. Once there was an Irishman, someone had told him that he could find work near Eagle Bridge. But he had forgotten the name eagle, and as they had no eagles in Ireland, and as he knew it was a large bird, it would have to be a hawk; so he went along the road asking everyone he met, could they be after telling him where there was a bridge with a hawk on it. Then for many years it was called the bridge with the hawk on it.

❖

Back in my childhood days, while staying at Vandenbergs', I went to school with a girl of my own age, Jessie Van Rensselaer. The Van Rensselaers were our next neighbors, they were thrifty farmers. On hot days I would go over to the Van Rensselaer farm to see Jessie. We would take out our lunch in the backyard and sit on a rock to eat it, with our bare feet dangling in the cool brook that ran through what now is our lawn. In those days little did I ever think that thirty odd years later I would make my home with my family on what years ago had been the Van Rensselaer farm.

While living in Staunton our home was called Mt. Nebo. And when we came back to New York State the children wanted to call the new home Mt. Nebo, they thought it very appropriate, and so it is. It was my home in 1905, and still is, there are many changes, but still my home.

❖

My husband and I just dropped back to where we had left off. We commenced to settling the first night we moved in. Each one said, "I'm going to have that room,"

[102]

and "I'm going to have that room," and I said "I'm going to have that room," and Thomas, he wanted this room because it looked right out to Hoosick Falls. Ona wanted the big room, and Loyd and Forrest had what is the bathroom now, and the two other little rooms were used as storage rooms, they didn't look inviting to the kids. I let each one pick his room, and then it was all theirs.

The first night we put mattresses and feather beds on the floor; then the girls and boys got their beds up. It was quite cold but not bad yet, we didn't have cold weather early that year. Mother wanted us to come up to her, till we'd get settled, but I thought after we got started, it would be better to stay down here, so we did.

We could not settle much till after the holidays, so many would come to see Thomas and Mary. All of Thomas' people—and he had a lot of them—had to come to see him, and see the children. As for the children, my family made too much of them. They were called "rebels," because they believed in the South, in the theories down there. Their Yankee cousins didn't know anything about all that, and it caused a kind of family feud; they never did get along too well—they had not been used to having cousins.

Thomas went to his brother who had hunted him up a western horse in the Falls. The other he got right here, to make up a team. As soon as they got those going, they commenced with the work. The first thing they did was to get a lot of wood for the following summer, to cut it up with the saw—that was farmer's work in those days.

Then we commenced regular work, getting the chickens in order, getting them to laying. After the holidays the children commenced to go to school near-by. Winona, the oldest, did not go, she helped me to paint and paper the house through, and settle the rooms. Then, in the spring she went to the Albany Business School for a year; she was very capable and smart in all things.

Thomas had bought up a herd of cows, and commenced to sell milk. He was happy to be back home; as for me I was first very homesick, it seemed to me as though I was down in a swamp all the time; while in Virginia we were 1600 feet above sea level, here we are only 300 feet above. Some call this a pretty valley, but give me the Shenandoah Valley, every time!

❖

We had not been here more than ten days and were eating dinner, when somebody rapped on the door and Ona went and opened it; there was a boy that I knew before I went South, and he asked for Anna Mary. He'd always come to our house and played the violin, it was nice music and we weren't used to it. He was sweet on my sister Celestia, that was the reason he came. Ona came back, she was scared at such a fine looking man asking for me. He came right in and caught hold of my hand and said, "Oh, I am so glad to see you, Anna Mary." Thomas was taken so by surprise, that was the only time he ever was jealous, he thought there was something between Martin and me. But Martin thought a great deal of Celestia, she was his girl.

I never was friendly with any boy except my husband. Oh, we'd go to the country dances, but the next day I would feel so mean and dirty from dancing with this one and that one. They were just dances to entertain and spend the evening, somebody would play the harmonica, anything for fun, it whiled away the time. In my father's house they played dominos or checkers, but no cards, he would not have that. If he found a pack around the hired man, he'd take it right into the stove and say nothing. If mother reproved it, he'd say, "The devil's in the cards." He also would not have anyone around cussing. Mother thought it was on account of Lester, but he could swear to beat the band before he was 10, but he got over it.

They didn't sit up late nights, in most houses 9 o'clock was bed hour, and half after 5 o'clock they'd get up.

Life on the Farm

Well time passed on, on a farm the days are nearly all the same, nothing changes but the seasons. In the early morning, before the sun was up, I would dress and build the fire, and put on the tea kettle for hot water, go out to the hen house, feed and water the chickens, come in and get breakfast, calling all hands to the table. By this time the men have finished the milking, and the horses have been curried and fed, ready for work. Coffee and hot cakes are all ready, now we have breakfast. Then for five to six long hours in the field and in the house. Then a good dinner and back to work again till sun down, then supper and the milking; and then with some there would be a reading of a chapter in the Bible and a prayer, then to bed till another day.

Life was a sort of routine. Monday washday, Tuesday ironing and mending, Wednesday baking and cleaning, Thursday sewing, Friday sewing and odd jobs, such as working in the garden or with the flowers. We did all of our own sewing, cleaning, papering, painting—we were thrifty farmers. In the spring, there were the maple trees to be tapped, so as to have syrup and sugar, then to boil up a barrel of soft soap to last the year through. And now house cleaning time comes on, and before that is finished, it is time to gather small fruit; in between, the housework must be kept up. All this is supposed to be cared for by the women and children. Then there is more or less sickness in a large family, but no doctor unless death comes stalking in your door, we depended on home nursing.

Then in the spring after the corn was planted, and a circus came to town, the boys would have a day off for recreation. The girls had to wait for summer picnics. Later there would be fairs for older people. And farmers and their wives were supposed to furnish produce for the fair.

And thus it was from year to year.

The Children

Loyd didn't like school. The teacher was not a lady, he said. Why wasn't she a lady? Well, there was a strange dog came in one day, and she kicked the dog, and no lady would ever kick a dog, he said. He went there a couple of winters, and then he went out to the Alfred Agricultural School. Forrest went to Hoosick Falls, and Anna too.

Anna had a nice disposition, kind and full of fun. She always drew a crowd, when she was here, always some fun going on, I never minded her friends; we had our three meals a day, whatever it was, and they were always welcome. I would have a lot of bread and always had a jar of sugar cookies and ginger cookies.

I used sometimes to bake a nice loaf cake every week, on the two top shelves I would keep the pie and cake. But when I had a nice cake, and I would go to the cupboard to get it, it wouldn't be there, the boys had gotten there ahead of me. So I got a strap iron in the stable and put a lock and key on it. Then I was safe for a week or so. Then, one day, I had a chocolate cake in there, and it wasn't there. The door was locked, but there was no cake in the cupboard. We had to go without it. The boys had gone and gotten the coal chisel and pried the staples from under the hook of the lock. It was on for some days till I discovered that the lock had gotten loose. I would scold them, but they said, "Oh well, it was good, better than it would ever taste again," and a dozen excuses; what could I say, they were hungry and they liked it!

I never really scolded my children. I used to whip the boys when they were little in the South, but when I'd whip one, I'd whip them all, so they couldn't make sport of the other one. I used to make them cut their own switches, from the lilac bushes, that was half the punishment. I never whipped hard, like I've seen children whipped in those days. They were pretty good, mine, always.

I don't think I ever lost my temper and got real wild like some folks, even when I was young. When I get angry, I just keep quiet, and think "Ishkabibble"—what the meaning of "Ishkabibble" is I don't know, but it's quite a by-word, something like "the devil take you." If you lose your temper, you do something and say something which you wouldn't if you waited a few minutes. (But a flash of temper is sometimes better than to brood over things and feel revengeful, that kind of pries on your mind when you get like that.)

❖

The children were always full of pranks, always in mischief with their young friends. One summer the two Reel sisters, whose brother Loyd had met at school, boarded with me for two or three weeks, and of all the frolics and mischief they got into! One day at the dinner table, after Thomas had gone out, someone threw water, then someone else. Then the battle was on, some were running out of doors, out to the pump and commenced to throw it by the bucket-full. Some ran upstairs for protection, and they threw water out of the window, nearly drowning the ones under the window. The battle grew hotter, and they threw the water into the window till it ran down the back-stairs into the dining room. Then one of the sisters said, she would not stand for it if she was me. I told her to let them have fun while they were young and could, it would be something to laugh about when they were old—and now they do.

It was a rollicksome, happy house, and their father would join in with them, he really was one of them.

❖

My parents both died in the year 1909. Mother died on February 24th, hers was heart trouble, she was only 69. Father was twenty years older than mother, his funeral was the twelfth of June. He was pretty well up till the last few months. He would come here to see us and walk all the way down. Thomas would always try to take him back to Oak Hill, but if it wasn't convenient, he would walk back again.

The pictures that were taken of mother were very good. She had a stern look, but she was full of fun and jokes, and she remembered so many things, which she taught me. She had a dark brown hair, and her eyes were something like mine, a grey green, she never was rosy but had an olive skin. They used to claim that I favor the Robertsons, but as I grow older, I can see mother's face in mine. The picture I had taken last spring was so much like mother looked when I went South.

❖

After Forrest graduated here in the Falls, he went out to Syracuse for two terms, in 1914. He became a good judge of cattle, a lover of refinement. We sent Loyd to Alfred University for three terms, and Anna to New York to study for nurse. Hugh was the baby in those days, he was still in school here, he had a great memory.

I used to cook the food and send it to all the children; every week I sent bread and rolls, cakes and pies. They could make their own coffee and fry their own cakes. They had to pay board, but getting the food from home made it much more reasonable for them. The boys came back home after they got through and went to help their father out with the farm work. They farmed different here than they did in the South. Loyd got new ideas and still gets them, he tries to keep up on new things, not like the old farmers who are in no hurry to take on new methods. He understood things far beyond his years.

[109]

They considered this here quite a model farm. There was the orchard, and at that time it was doing fine, lots of work, but it used to pay our taxes; of course, they weren't quite so high as they are now.

❖

They had little machinery in those days, but the iron age came on very fast. In 1913 we bought our first car, an Overland, that gave the young folks lots of pleasure, and the Yankee cousins thought more of the "rebels."

It was the year of 1907, I remember seeing a balloon going over from Argyle to Cambridge, N. Y., there was a man, woman and child in it. They landed in Cambridge. In 1911 there was lots of talk about a new invention, airplanes. Sometime later I saw my first. And my first movie I saw in Syracuse in 1914, that was grand.

Much has changed since my mother, back in the year 1865, had sperm oil lamps. One day father brought home a jug of kerosene, nearly all were afraid of it. Father poured some into a saucer and held a match to it, but it would not burn. Then he poured some water into it, then it blazed up and burned. I think it was in 1913 I saw the first electric lights in Albany, although it might have been gas as well. It was along 1936 or 7 when we got electric light in the house.

Luke Carpenter

We had an old friend, Luke Carpenter, a very nice man of the old Yankee stock. The Carpenters came here from

Rhode Island in the year of 1790 or there about, Mr. Carpenter coming first, and took up a tract of land over in the Hoosick Hills. He built himself a log cabin, and a bob sleigh, then got himself a yoke of oxen. Then he went back to Rhode Island to get him a wife; she came down here sitting on the bob sleigh on a chair that her husband had made, while he drove the oxen through the wilderness, that must have been in the year 1800. They were a large family, some of them still got the chair that their grandma rode in on her wedding trip.

These were the grandparents of our friend Luke. They all were wonderful cabinet makers, they made all of their chairs, I have an old Boston rocker that Luke made many years ago; the slats in the back are built out of the fingers of a grain cradle such as you reap grain with.

We loved to hear Luke tell of olden times, it was better than television is today, and we all would have such good laughs at his stories. He didn't like the automobiles, he had a horse and buggy, and he would get into the middle of the road when he heard them coming—"devil catchers," he would call them. And when he heard that any of the young people in the neighborhood were going to get married, he would make a molding board, a potato masher and a rolling pin, that was his present, he enjoyed doing it. He loved to go to clambakes, but he could not eat the clams, they were too tough, so he would take along his meat grinder, and screw it on the table beside his plate, and grind his clams so he could eat them. He was a true American, had a mind of his own.

My brother Joe's wife Edna had tuberculosis, she was very sick. My sister Celestia used to go over to them about one day a week, to help. Edna's father was also there, he had been cooking the meals for Joe and the children, he was a good cook. They had five children, Eleanor was the baby, about a year old, and there was another girl, Florence, about seven years old, and three boys. I used to clean up Edna's room, and Celestia did some of the washing and ironing.

One day Celestia came down and said, "Edna won't last long, hadn't we better go down and straighten up the house?" And she said, "When Edna is gone, which one of the children are you going to take?" I said, "If I take any of them, I take the baby, but I don't think that Joe will give up any of them." "Well," she said, "I want Florence." Celestia's girl was about the same age.

Edna didn't live more than a day after that. Then Celestia did take Florence, so that she went to school with Margaret, but she didn't undertake to keep her, Joe didn't want to give her up. Joe had to go out to do his farming work, so he had to leave the little girl Eleanor in the care of the little boys. One day, when Celestia happened to go over there, she found the baby sitting out in the chip pile, where they cut wood, playing with the boys, she could sit alone at that time. So she took the baby home that night. Anna and I happened to go up to Celestia the next day, and I found my baby up there. And nothing would do but Anna had to bring the baby down home with her, she was going to take care of her. She couldn't talk yet. That's how Eleanor came here in the first place.

Then I wrote a letter to Joe and how come I had his baby, but any time he wanted her back, he should come and get her. And I would bring her up anyway in a few days. But then we got attached to her, and they kind of weaned away from her there, it gave them freedom, and we didn't mind taking care of her here. She was a very good, fat baby.

She stayed till she got married. She had a good home here, and of her uncle Thomas she thought more than she did of anybody else.

The Children Leave Home

And then the children got married and went to homes of their own. In the year 1910, on November 28, our daughter Winona was married to Jack Fisher, an engineer in the State Service. The wedding was here in the house. Ed Tibbitts was the minister who married them. Sister Ona, and Mrs. Hayden and Mrs. Miller came over from North Adams, and Mrs. Miller helped with the dinner. She wanted a large vessel to make the coffee in, and I said, "I guess you have the largest vessel, unless you want the wash boiler?" "Well, I guess I do want that. How many men's old socks have been boiled in it?" I told her, none at all, it was almost a new boiler. My sister Celestia came down and made the scalloped oysters and pressed chicken. Sister Ona attended to the cake. Aunt Mattie, Uncle Charlie, and Guy, brother Joe, uncle Fred and Georgia—all were there.

[113]

But there were none of my aunts, there would have been too many.

I had the house trimmed and the arch made in the parlor, a pillow underneath to kneel on. Rena Herrington helped trim up the room with autumn leaves and bittersweet, and the flowers were dahlias. You didn't buy flowers then; they had a wagon load of bittersweet. I made a white cake, and a dark cake, and one large cake they called the bride's cake. Jack had to do the cutting. There must have been about 50 here, 16 at each table; but I didn't have so much on my hands with all the help I had. It was a nice wedding.

Ona's wedding outfit I had made in the fall before. It was a creamy white satin, very pretty, nobody would believe that I made it, but it wasn't any more than if I had made a cotton one. Evelyn Herrington played the wedding march; she started, when Ona was coming down to the parlor. Ona had played on that piano, she took lessons when she was little, and the piano was gotten for her. Those who have been here and understand music said it had a wonderful tone; it needs retuning now. The old man who tuned it for us in the South, before we came up here, said he worked in that factory when he was a boy, and he told us it was over 100 years old. It was made in Alexandria, Va.

We just had the dinner and the ceremony, and then all went home. They all took the half after three to New York. The house was empty before candle-light. I didn't mind it so much, I had lots of dishes to wash.

❖

In the year 1915 we bought a large farm for the two boys, it had a lot of sheep on it; they commenced to work it that spring with their father's help and boarded at home till the spring of 1916, when Forrest got married, then they were on their own. The same fall Loyd married. They married two sisters, Mary Brown, Forrest's wife, Alice Brown, Loyd's wife. They lived in a two-family house. Forrest's and Loyd's weddings were down at their wives' home. Mary wore a white dress, it was quite short, she looked like a little girl going to school. There is some place in the text, "With all my worldly goods I thee endow." Mary said, she looked up on the hill and saw Forrest's sheep, and she thought he would have to give her those sheep! She had thirteen garters given to her, and she had to wear them. That was for the number of children they were supposed to have. They were fancy garters like men used to wear on their shirt sleeves. It was for good luck, just like you should wear "something new, something old, something borrowed, something stoled."

❖

Loyd was "Good Man Friday" until Forrest was married. Forrest was always the boss, like Robinson Crusoe, and Friday was the Come-Hither man. When they were little boys, their father had a pile of corn on the corn house floor, and he had told the boys to throw it into the bin. Loyd went at it just as quick as he could, and was willing as a beaver. Forrest, he straightened up after a little bit and said, "I'll be dead in a thousand years." He didn't like to work.

The Runaway

One summer my sister Ona came to visit me and she wanted to take a ride back to her old home, so we planned the day. I had the work all done up in the early morning, the dinner about finished for the men folks, and my youngest daughter said she could finish it. So I asked my husband to hitch Topsy, the driving horse, to the surrey, and we would go for a ride. I dressed my little niece Eleanor, then I dressed myself in a very pretty green and white batiste dress, and we drove away, my husband said, "Take good care of yourselves, I wished I could go with you."

We had a lovely day and drive, and had turned to come home. Sister got out to hitch the horse, and Eleanor was on the ground. As sister pulled off the bridle, Topsy plunged and whirled, taking the surrey almost over little Eleanor's head. I grabbed the lines, but away we went, a real runaway, two miles in less than a few minutes, they told me later. I thought I could stop Topsy, but I realized she had no bridle on, and I was holding her up by the breast strap, but I did not dare let up for fear Topsy would tangle and fall, so on we went down through the long woods. There I met two men in a buckboard, we clicked wheels, but I did not stop, oh no! I was going somewhere. . . . I knew I had a half mile of down grade and then two sharp turns and acrost a bridge. Now, if I can only make the turns, I think, Topsy will stop as there was a long steep hill to go up. Well, I made the first turn by leaning all to one side of the surrey, but before I got to the next turn, I saw the

Grandma's painting table

Grandma at the age of ninety-one

wheels going under, just as we struck the bridge—and then no more for a while.

How I left the surrey, I'll never know; the first thing I did know, I was trying to get my head out of a dirty slimy mud pond. Oh, but I was a sight! Covered with that green frog moss from the top of my head to the sole of my feet! I had lost my hat and my glasses, and was soaking wet, standing in about two feet of mud and water. I thought, oh where is that horse? I must find it, so I started for the road which was about eight feet above the mud puddle. I tried to climb the bank, but my knees would not work, so I tried to pull myself up the bank with the grass, but one hand was no good, could not shut my fingers. After a time I made out to crawl up the bank and get on my feet. And there stood Topsy, but the surrey was on its side, too heavy to run with any more. I commenced to pray if I could only reach that horse before it starts up again, so I was hobbling towards it. Two men were coming acrost a field, so I called to them, "Don't scare her, get her by the nose, she is gentle." One of the men asked me if I was hurt, I said, "Oh, no, I'm all right." "But your face is covered with blood," they said, and I thought it was water. I had cut my nose.

Well, the men set the surrey on its wheels, shook it a few times, then wanted that I should go up to their home and get on some dry clothes. The men that I had passed in the woods, had turned around, "to pick up the corpse," they said. Now they were willing to help, so I sent them back to pick up my sister and niece. Someone had sent for a doctor and by the time we got up to the house, he was there. He found me badly bruised and a broken arm, things I had not found out.

Well, in a week's time the runaway was forgotten, for evermore. . . .

❖

In 1917, Ona's husband enrolled in officer's training. Next year he went across to Europe, they broke up householding, and Ona sent all her things up here. Jack told his father he was going to enlist. They were German people, so his father said, "All right, but if you are going over, you're going to fight your own cousins." When he was ready to go over, Ona went into the Navy. She was there until he came home. But he was shell shocked, it was some time before he could do anything. He couldn't stand it in New York, he was in very bad condition, he couldn't trust himself, he said. As soon as there was any commotion going on, he would go all to pieces. But Ona had to stay in New York, she was still in the Navy, she couldn't live anywhere else. So they agreed to disagree, Jack went to Syracuse, I hear from him now and then.

❖

After Anna graduated from high school, she went to Hunter College in New York City, then she took up nursing at St. Luke's Hospital.

The day before Jack came home from the war, Anna had a hemorrhage in the hospital where she was studying. She was perfectly well, and this night she was going through

[118]

the nurses' hall, they were talking and joking, and there was one tall nurse, who was boasting how strong she was, and Anna just came in the door with a tray. This nurse set her tray away and took Anna and turned her right around, upside down, until somebody interfered. "I seemed to be all right," Anna said, "but everything seemed to have gone to my throat." She took up the tray and went on. After a time she went to bed and in that night she was taken with this hemorrhage, a hemorrhage from the lungs. I didn't know until the next day. They put her out on a sleeping porch. A specialist waited on her two or three days, and then he said, if she has got any folks, get her home. He had done all he could, like, there is no hopes. But, of course, he didn't let her know that. Ona couldn't leave the Navy, so she asked Jack if he couldn't take Anna home. That's the first we knew that he was home. He phoned up to Loyd to meet him at such a train over here at the depot and to have Dr. Shaw there. They all came together, and I brought Anna up, she walked up the stairs, I didn't know what condition she was in. I put her right to bed, she said, "They say I must stay in bed." She kept getting better, I had both windows out, it was just like a sleeping porch, ideal place, and she had to be kept quiet for a long time and be well fed. I think she stayed in bed for about six weeks, I fed her the best I could think of. She got along nicely, and after she got real well, she was still determined to be a nurse. She took up domestic nursing in Albany. In 1922 she was back home again and taught school for a term here at Waite's Corners. The next summer aunt Zoe, uncle Walter's wife, had a shock, and they sent for Anna to help. She was there when her aunt died. She stayed on and kept house for uncle Walter and her cousin Frank. They were always sweet on each other, Frank and Anna. Frank always thought there was no one like Anna, and she thought he was pretty good. In February 1924 they took a trip to New York and were married in the little Church around the Corner. And then uncle Walter built them a house in the yard and Anna moved into it before it was quite finished, because if they did not get in at a certain time, they would have to pay taxes for a number of years. That was up in Bennington, on Elm Street. She must have been there about seven years.

❖

Hugh was married to Dorothy Harrison before he was twenty. They were married in the Episcopal Church in Hoosick Falls, just two or three went along for the ceremony. They went to Schroon Lake on their wedding trip, and then they came right back home to live with us.

❖

At that time I cooked and washed for the whole family, I had a Hammer washing machine that was hand-operated. When wash day came, I often thought over the verses that were in our reading book in school long ago:

> Oh Monday was our washing day, and while
>   the clothes were drying,
> A wind came whistling through the line and
>   set them all a'flying.
> I saw the shirts and petticoats go flying off
>   like witches,

I lost, oh bitterly I wept, I lost my Sunday
    breeches,
I saw them flying through the air, alas, too late
    to save them,
A hole was in their ample part, as if an imp had
    worn them.

In my childhood days, on Monday morning, bright and
early, we would get up the wash bench, two wooden tubs,
rubbing board and pounding barrel and two pails from the
cellar, that was our washing machine through all the years.
We carried the water from a spring a long ways from the
house and were thankful to have that. And a large, snow-
white wash would be floating on the wind by eleven o'clock,
if we were not lazy folks.

All the refrigerators we had in those days, was a very deep
well, where we would place perishable food in a large basket
or tin can, and lower it down into the well by rope or
chain, such as butter, or cream for churning.

❖

I voted for the first time before Anna went away from
home. I think women should vote, they have to make a living just the same as the men do, so why should they not have
a say-so? Some women are more capable holding office than
some men are. They can belong home, but to keep up the
home they should have a say how it is run. Since women
commenced to vote, they have more freedom. They don't
have the drudgery they used to have, too. With education
and voting, they have more to say how the children should

go to school. If they are going to have a career, they should have a career, but let the family business alone. They cannot fill both places.

❖

I never taught my children anything like those common jingles, we used to sing, they didn't care for that kind of songs, they were more modern, they liked songs like "Going out to the ball game," Mother Gooses and such things. I sang lots of songs by heart, I still know them, the old darkie songs, they were quite a rage, like the "Suwannee River," "Kitty Well," "Nelly Grey," or "Old Kentucky Home." With the tune you do catch on to things quickly. When I was a child, we used to play a game that everybody had to have some certain song for entertainment. Irish songs went over good at that time.

❖

One time I was papering the parlor, and I ran short of paper for the fire board. So I took a piece of paper and pasted it over the board, and I painted it a solid color first, then I painted two large trees on each side of it, like butternut trees. And back in it I did a little scene of a lake and painted it a yellow color, really bright, as though you were looking off into the sun light. In the front, to fill in that space, I brought in big bushes. I daubed it all on with the brush I painted the floor with. Dorothy's grandfather, when he saw it, he made a great to-do, "Oh, isn't that beautiful, that's the most wonderful thing I ever see, don't let anything happen to that!" he said. It run on three or four years, and we

[122]

re-papered the parlor and papered over the picture. When we re-papered the room again a few years ago, Dorothy remembered the picture, and we took the paper off the fire board, but the colors had faded somewhat.

That was my first large picture.

Dark Days

It was a troubled day, that January 15th, 1927, a regular blizzard outside. About 10 o'clock Thomas had gone for wood, and I thought he would bring up some. When he came back and didn't have the wood, I said, "Thomas, are you sick?" He was always subject to headaches. "No," he said, "but I'm so cold." It was an awful cold day. I had a good fire in the stove, and I said, "Sit right down by the fire, I'll make you some ginger tea, and take off your boots." I went downstairs to make the tea, and I came up with the ginger tea; he stood with his back against the stove pipe, he had not changed his place. He did sit down and then lied down on the bed and took off his boots, I set the boots against the wall. "Thomas, do you mean you carry those boots all the time?" And I said, "I hope you never have to wear those heavy boots again!" I thought they were too heavy for anybody to carry around. He went off to sleep, and he must have slept about three hours with his clothes on, just as he was. I was baking bread, and I went down to finish it off to get it ready for the oven. He had been wearing one of those plaid wool jackets, and it was quite dirty, so I thought I'd take it down and wash it, and I did so. When I came back, I said, "Anything you would like to eat?" He says, "No, but you might bring me a cup of tea

[123]

and put some sugar in it, that last cup was so bitter." I probably was in the kitchen about an hour and left the bread for Dorothy to finish. I brought the tea and the lamp— it was about 4 o'clock and quite dark. "Take the tea," I said, "and here is a clean jacket for you." And he says, "It's dark." I said, "Yes, it's been dark all day." As I set the lamp down and I lit it, as I did that, he made a funny noise, like a person kind of choking, and said, "It turned dark all at once." Those were his last words.

I had a frightened feeling, I spoke to him, "Thomas, I managed to put on the light." I heard Hugh going to his room to get his wood, and told him to come at once. "He ought to have a doctor," he said, and he started out. He had to go to a neighbor and phone from there to the Falls for Doctor Shaw. I came back into the room and went to Thomas, and I knew the minute I got back he was gone. Then I ran downstairs and asked if Hugh had left, and I said, "Father Moses has gone."

There was nothing we could do. Pretty soon Loyd and Forrest came. They said the doctor was not home, but he would come just as quick as he could. By the time they all were in, Dr. Shaw came. He said, "If I had been right here, I couldn't have saved him." It was angina of the heart. He never knew that he was going. And yet, he made some very strange remarks that fall.

Once he said, "I don't mind dying." I said, "You are not going to die, you are perfectly well!" "Well, I wouldn't mind, but then I think I'd rather think of you lying under the snow. I can't bear the thought, to go and leave you here." "Why, Thomas," I said, "I took care of myself a good many years before you ever knew me." "I know," he said, "that would be different now, if you were left alone. But if there

[124]

is such a thing as coming back to this earth, I will come back and watch over you." Just as though he seemed to know that he was going.

❖

I had always liked to paint, but only little pictures for Christmas gifts and things like that. Thomas had never talked about my painting, he thought it was foolish. But one night, a few weeks before his death, he came in, it was after candlelight, and he asked, "Who did that painting?" And I thought it was one of my sister's paintings, so I said, "I don't know, must be one of my sister's." He said, "That's really good, that behind the stove." Then I knew that it was the one I had just painted for Edward, "A little blue boy beside the fence." "Oh," I said, "that isn't much." "No, that's real good." And then he just couldn't keep away the last few weeks, when I started to do a little painting, he was right there watching and liked it so much.

I am not superstitious or anything like that. But there is something like an overruling power. I never thought that I would do such work, I never know how I'm going to paint until I start in; something tells me what to go right on and do. It was just as though he had something to do about this painting business. I have always thought ever since, I wonder if he has come back, I wonder if he is watching over me.

❖

On Christmas 1932 Anna got the flu and I went up to take care of her, but she got well soon, and had company come in and was talking and laughing and showing some pictures she had taken of the children. She had just handed one of the pictures to one of the ladies to see, and I was cutting out a garment on the table, Anna hopped right up and said something and started for the bathroom, and I saw her hand up to her mouth, as she went past me. She had been taken with a hemorrhage. She got into the bathroom, lost her breath and started out onto the porch, and was about to fall on account of her breath. Just this moment Frank had driven into the yard. I was holding her up, and he and his helper came running into the house, and called the doctor. He came and gave her icepacks, then she got pneumonia. She only lived a few days after that.

Anna was buried in the burying grounds in Bennington in uncle Walter's lot. I never could find her grave, when I have gone there, she had no stone of her own. They keep the ground there as level as they possibly can, on account of mowing it. They got a monument there now for the whole family.

I stayed on, right from that time, for two years, until Frank got married again. I took care of the house and the two children, the same as I would have at home.

Before Anna died, she had promised Frances a birthday party, and after she was gone we gave her the birthday party just the same.

The two children went through high school, and Zoan became a trained nurse. She is married and living in Colorado. Frances is working in a laboratory as a biologist.

A Visit to the South

I went down South visiting once, with Forrest, Mary and Betty, my oldest grandchild. We must have gone in November, after the work was done up. Forrest kept going west all the time, and I told him, that wasn't right, that Virginia was south of us, but he knew just how to go, and we got to Staunton. We stayed there for about a week and had a very pleasant visit, went out nearly to West Virginia one day, and over east another day, towards Richmond, and called on all of our old neighbors. They were mostly all living at that time. We drove around to see the old places and the bridges, the fords were done away with, they didn't have them any more on account of the cars. The Dudley place, we couldn't cross that ford, we had to go way off by the woods, and there was a bridge. Some of the places looked just as we left them, some were all changed, and the meadow that we used to cross going over to the chapel was all built over with factories, you wouldn't know the country. They had an air port there.

Forrest visited around with his old school mates, but Mary was glad to go back, she never likes to be away from home.

Arthritis

When Zoan was a baby, Anna asked me one day to make her a worsted picture, she had seen one and liked it, and thought I could do one better. Well, I tried it, and it was a success, so I made many a picture, and gave away many of these. But then my hands were getting tired and lame, I could not handle a large needle any more. It was chronic rheumatism, I used to wrap my hands up in scarves and lay them on a chair beside the bed, at night I couldn't sleep on account of the aching, just like a tooth ache. Then, one night I got desperate, so I got up and hunted the doctor book, the "Family Adviser, Philosophy of Diseases." The best recipe was: 3 cups of sweet milk every day, and from 3 to 5 drops of turpentine in it. I took it for about three months, and all of a sudden there were no pains any more, but the hardness of the joints stayed.

That was the only doctor book I had in the house. It belonged to William King, my father's uncle, and he had this book, when they went to the gold rush in California. He went there as the doctor. He was the only doctor, and they started across the Isthmus of Panama. There he died. His friend who was with him gathered up his things and shipped them back to his mother. The date, 1834, in the book, is when he wrote his name in it. It was printed in 1833 by Henry Wilkins. My sister Sarah, when she was little, got hold of the book and drew a picture on the last page. It was supposed to be my parents' home, Oak Hill. She was a great hand at drawing with a pencil, it was a natural gift for her. She sometimes said to Hugh, when he was little, "Come on, Hugh, if I draw a picture, will you go to bed?" Then she drew a picture, just as perfect as could be in just a few minutes, then he'd go to bed. Sarah died when she was in her thirties. My sister Celestia also painted. She took lessons when she was about 16 or 18, she was a beautiful painter, but she never did much of it.

Painting

As for myself, I started to paint in my old age, one might say, though I had painted a few pictures before. My sister Celestia came down one day and saw my worsted pictures and said: "I think you could paint better and faster than you could do worsted pictures." So I did, and painted for pleasure, to keep busy and to pass the time away, but I thought of it no more than of doing fancy work.

When I had quite a few paintings on hand, someone suggested that I send them down to the old Thomas' drug store in Hoosick Falls, so I tried that. I also exhibited a few at the Cambridge Fair with some canned fruits and raspberry jam. I won a prize for my fruit and jam, but no pictures.

And then, one day, a Mr. Louis J. Caldor of New York City, an engineer and art collector, passing through the town of Hoosick Falls, saw and bought my paintings. He wanted to know who had painted them, and they told him it was an old woman that was living down on the Cambridge Road by the name of Anna Mary Moses. So when I came home that night, Dorothy said: "If you had been here, you could have sold all your paintings, there was a man here looking for them, and he will be back in the morning to see them. I told him how many you had." She thought I had about ten, something like that.

Well, I didn't sleep much that night, I tried to think where I had any paintings and what they were, I knew I didn't have many, they were mostly worsted, but I thought, towards morning, of a painting I had started on after house cleaning days, when I found an old canvas and frame, and

[129]

I thought I had painted a picture on it of Virginia. It was quite large, and I thought if I could find frames in the morning I could cut that right in two and make two pictures, which I did, and by so doing I had the ten pictures for him when he came. I did it so it wouldn't get Dorothy in the dog house. But he didn't discover the one I had cut in two for about a year, then he wanted to know what made me cut my best picture in two. I told him, it's just Scotch thrift.

He wanted me to paint more, he came back several times, he bought the pictures and paid for them. He took them down to New York to show in the galleries, three of these found their way into a Museum of Modern Art exhibition. Then in October of 1940 I had the first exhibit of my paintings placed at the Galerie St. Etienne, 46 West 57th Street. When my exhibition opened large numbers of elderly people came having heard my story.

The Big City

Then there was a request for me to go to the big city, New York, for a Thanksgiving celebration in Gimbels' auditorium, where they had hung the Grandma Moses pictures. Grandma, who had never travelled much—what anticipation and vexation, what commotion and confusion, at last she was on her way!

They wanted me to take down some preserves and some home-made bread and cake. My preserves were placed on the tables beside the platform. Just before I went up there with Mrs. Thomas, someone handed me one of those little old ladies' bouquets and then someone pinned something on me, it felt just like a black bug, but I couldn't look down. It was a microphone, I was on the air. They took me by surprise, I was in from the back woods, and I didn't know what they were up to. So while I thought I was talking to Mrs. Thomas, I spoke to four hundred people at the Thanksgiving Forum in Gimbels' auditorium.

Afterwards, oh it was shake hands, shake, shake, shake—and I wouldn't even know the people now. My, my, it was rush here, rush there, rush every other place—but I suppose I shouldn't say that, because those people did go to so much bother to make my visit pleasant.

❖

That winter I had the grippe, and they kept me in bed, and I planned mischief then. When I was lying there, I thought I was going to paint the story of the "Old Oaken Bucket," because I knew how it originated. I painted it when I got up, that was the first one I tried, but later I painted it again and could remember more of the details.

Then I was requested to send several pictures out to the gallery in Syracuse, where they had an exhibition. I sent the "Old Oaken Bucket," the "Checkered House," and a picture with a young colt in it. Hugh and Dorothy persuaded me to attend the show, so we went to Syracuse. My picture, "The Old Oaken Bucket," took the New York State Prize, and Mr. Thomas J. Watson bought it. That was in May 1941.

My Tip-up Table

Painting is a very pleasant hobby, if one does not have to hurry, I love to take my time and finish things up right.

I have an old tip-up table, on which I paint. My aunt gave it to me thirty-five years ago, it was built for a log cabin. Back in the 18th century, Phinious Whiteside came and made his home in the township of Washington County, New York, taking up a tract of land, on which he made his home. He had a large family of girls and boys. When his oldest son became of age he gave him his portion, which was the custom in those days, a freedom suit, so many sheep, an ax and I think 200 acres of land, and said, now go and build a home for yourself. He went into the 200 acres of heavy timber which joined his father's, cut down trees and built himself a bed, and a trundlebed, then the tip-back table, so as when the trundlebed was run out, there would be room enough to move about. The table was made of pine planks, under the top between the standards there was a box in which they kept their pewter dishes, this had a plank cover so that it formed a chair. Long years after the new large brick house was built, the table was moved over into the cellar and used as a milk table for many more years. Then one day my aunt sent it to me for a flower stand; I have painted scenes on the standards and covered the top with postal cards, and now use it for my easel.

How I Paint

When I first commenced to paint with oil, I thought every painting would be my last one, so I was not so interested. Then the requests commenced to come for this one and that one. "Paint me one just like that one!" so I have painted on and on, till now. I think I am doing better work than at first, but it is owing to better brushes and paint. The brushes help greatly, I can get now little brushes, I couldn't get at one time during the war, sometimes I had to use a match. And the colors now are good, and then I got so that I can mix them and do better work with them.

Before I start painting, I get a frame, then I saw my masonite board to fit the frame. (I always thought it a good idea to build the sty before getting the pig, likewise with young men, get the home before the wedding.)

Then I go over the board with linseed oil, then with three coats of flat white paint to cover up the darkness of the board. With two coats, the dark would strike through in some places, and three give it body, so when you start to paint the picture, you don't have to put on so much of the colored paint. The tube paint is quite expensive, and you have to use it accordingly, that's a Scotch idea, you see. Now the board is ready for the scene, whatever the mind may produce, a landscape, an old bridge, a dream, or a summer or winter scene, childhood memories, but always something pleasing and cheerful, I like bright colors and activity. I use masonite or hard wood to paint on, because it will last many years longer than canvas. Sometimes the frames are hard to obtain, they may be pretty frames, but in a dilapidated condition, then I must use hammer and nails and plastico. The frames should always blend with the paintings for best effect.

When I paint, I study and study the outside lots of times. Often I get at loss to know just what shade of green, and there are a hundred trees that have each three or four shades of green in them. I look at a tree and I see the limbs, and then the next part of the tree is a dark, dark black green, then I have got to make a little lighter green, and so on. And then on the outside, it'll either be a yellow green, or whitish green, that's the way the trees are shaded. And the snow—they tell me that I should shade it more or use more blue, but I have looked at the snow and looked at the snow, and I can see no blue, sometimes there is a little shadow, like the shadow of a tree, but that would be grey, instead of blue, as I see it. I love pink, and the pink skies are beautiful. Even as a child, the redder I got my skies with my father's old paint, the prettier they were.

On the Radio

The first radio I ever saw was a crystal set made by hand and given to Dorothy and Hugh for a Christmas present in 1920. The first time I had the experience of being on the radio myself was several years ago while I was in New York. There I met Bessie Beattie who asked me to go on the air at one of her broadcasts. I didn't think too much of this idea, but was glad to help her, so I accepted. The second time it was on the program "We the People," in April 1946. They had gone to a lot of trouble, sending two men from New York City. Carl Schutzman, an engineer, who came with a portable transmitting apparatus, was very patient listening for the switch-over to Eagle Bridge. Then there were four men from the Troy Telephone Company, to make connections between Grandma Moses and New York City.

I presume there were some nervous moments for those men who had gone to all that trouble and expense, for fear all would not go right. We found that we had but three minutes time allowed for the talk. Now who can say much in three minutes? So we had to boil it down to the three minutes.

The interview was with Mr. Gene Hurley, he was very nice and patient with me. We went over the program several times, I am a dumb Dora when it comes to such work, it is out of my line of business, but I enjoyed it, and I hope all the others did too. First I was asked, what kind of pictures I liked best, so I said, "I like pretty things the best, what's the use of painting a picture if it isn't something nice? So I think real hard till I think of something real pretty, and then I paint it. I like to paint old timey things, historical landmarks of long ago, bridges, mills and hostelries, those old time homes, there are a few left, and they are going fast. I do them all from memory, most of them are day dreams, as it were. . . ." Then he asked me, how it feels to be famous, and what I think of those millions of Christmas cards, made from my pictures. "Oh, I don't think about fame much, I keep my mind on what I am going to paint next, I have got a lot of catching up to do! And as to the Christmas cards, I can't think of much to say about them. My granddaughter out in Arizona jokes a lot about them, she says I am a witch, except I ride around the country on a paint brush, instead of a broom."

When all was over we had refreshments, then they all departed for their homes. Leaving the house so lonesome. . . .

Hugh Dies

February 10, 1949. I was upstairs in my room, and I heard Dorothy cry, "Oh no! oh no!" and wondered what had happened. I met Margy coming up, she was coming to drive me back. Edward said, "Don't let Grandma come!" I asked her what was the trouble, and she said, "Daddy is dead." I went right down to Dorothy and tried to quiet her down. I don't know whether I showed it that I was excited, I told Dorothy, "He is better off, he is with his father now."

Hugh, Edward and three other men had gone off towards Peru, Vermont that morning. They had got orders for long poles for the drive-in theatres and had them ready. Well, they got up to the load, and Edward went on one side of the logs and his father on the other side, to tighten the chains. Edward got a little ahead of his father and was wondering why his father wasn't catching the chain that he threw over, and he looked to see and saw his father lying on the ground, flat on his back, with the cigarette still smoking. He had dropped without knowing it.

Hugh was perfectly well, Dr. Shaw was in a few nights before, and he said later he thought he would be the last man that would go so soon. Like his father, he didn't know when he went, nor anything about it.

They brought him home that night or the next morning,

and then the flowers commenced to come in, the parlor was just full of flowers. He had a lot of friends.

Hugh is buried in the family lot in the Hoosick Falls cemetery.

Washington, D. C.

May 12, 1949. Leaving home with Dorothy for a trip to Washington, where I was to get an award from President Truman.

We were going by car to Albany, then we took the train for New York City. There they took me in a wheel chair and escorted me to a taxicab, that was humiliating to me, but I couldn't have walked it, such a long way from the train. Then we motored up to Riverside Drive, where we remained with Mr. and Mrs. Kallir till the 14th. Riding to Washington in a special car and arriving about three o'clock that day, we were escorted to the Hotel Statler. Here we were to have dinner with the Women's National Press Club, and there I received an award from the President.

Next day, Sunday, May 15th, we were gladly received by Mrs. Truman to a tea at the Blair House. After the tea we had a terrific thunderstorm, so we sat down on a couch to wait till the shower was over. President Truman sat beside me and said, "Don't be afraid, as this is a large building and has many lightning rods on it." Maybe he thought Grandma might be afraid. I talked with him, and I could not think but that he was one of my own boys. I even asked him to play something on the piano, which he did to pass the time away, that was a delight. Then the shower was over, and he ordered his own car to take us to the Hotel Statler, that was an honor.

The next day we went to Mount Vernon, and then we started home. Coming home, we were met by the largest crowd that has ever been in Eagle Bridge. It was all unexpected, the rest knew it, but I didn't. The children sang and presented me with a bunch of flowers. Alice said, "They'll expect you to make a speech," but I said, "Oh no, I will make no speech tonight." But I did have to thank them, as they all stood around me. The Hoosick Falls High School band played, and they escorted us home to a grand supper.

In a way I was glad to get back and go to bed that night.

❖

If I didn't start painting, I would have raised chickens. I could still do it now. I would never sit back in a rocking chair, waiting for someone to help me. I have often said, before I would call for help from outsiders, I would rent a room in the city some place and give pancake suppers, just pancake and syrup, and they could have water, like a little breakfast. I never dreamed that the pictures would bring in so much, and as for all that publicity, and as for the fame which came to Grandma so late, that I am too old to care for now. Sometimes it makes me think of a dream that my father once told at the breakfast table one morning many years ago. He said, "I had a dream about you last night, Anna Mary." "Was it good or bad, Pa?" And he said, "That depends on the future, dreams cast their shadows before us." He dreamed, I was in a large hall and there were many people there, they were clapping their hands and shouting and he wondered what it was all about. "And looking I saw you, Anna Mary, coming my way, walking on the shoulders of men; you came right on stepping from one shoulder to another, waving to me." Of late years I have often thought of that dream, since all the publicity about me, and of my mother saying to father, "Now, Russell, Anna Mary would look nice walking on men's shoulders!" She saw the folly of that dream. Or did that dream cast its shadows before? I often wonder, now that I am getting such kind well-wishing letters from almost every country on the globe.

❖ ❖
❖

In the foregoing chapters I have tried to tell you many true facts as they were in my days. It is hard in this age for one to realize how we grew up at all. I felt older when I was 16 than I ever did since. I was old and sedate when I left the Whitesides, I suppose it was the life I led, I had to be so lady-like. Even now I am not old, I never think of it, yet I am a grandmother to 11 grandchildren, I also have 17 great-grandchildren, that's a plenty!

Things have changed greatly and still are changing, can they change much more? Can you think of any more improvements? My father liked his fireplace the same as I like my old iron stove, and now they have the gas and electric ranges, but I would not be surprised, when the younger generation gets old, when people of coming generations, a hundred years from now, will look back upon us as primitives.

And yet I wonder sometimes whether we are progressing. In my childhood days life was different, in many ways, we were slower, still we had a good and happy life, I think, people enjoyed life more in their way, at least they seemed to be happier, they don't take time to be happy nowadays. But when you come to big questions like that, don't think too much, you must skip them, same as I did when I read the Bible to earn my silver thimble!

I have written my life in small sketches, a little today, a little yesterday, as I thought of it, as I remembered all the things from childhood on through the years, good ones, and unpleasant ones, that is how they come, and that is how we have to take them. I look back on my life like a good day's work, it was done and I feel satisfied with it. I was happy and contented, I knew nothing better and made the best out of what life offered. And life is what we make it, always has been, always will be.

REPRODUCTIONS
OF SOME LETTERS
BY GRANDMA MOSES

Autobiographical data from a letter which Grandma Moses wrote in answer to a questionnaire.

anna mary Robertson moses, EagleBridge, n.y,
Greenwich, was Co, year 1860,   5 feet one inch.
weight 140 pouns, eyes Hazel, Hair dark brown, gray now
marid, children, winona Robertson, Loyed Robert.
Forrest King, anna mary, Hugh worthinton,
are children studying art,   No,
Born. in state of n.y.   never studyed art,
I use Oil,
american art is beautifull, cheerfull and
greeting cards are very nice,   Hobbies I love all Kinds
woork,   am bury painting
receive no advice, "am a sorte no all"

Yes I think spring
is with us once
again,
I hear the blue
Birds and Robins
singing, and I
wants get out
of doors and
clean up,
It does lool bad
out there now,
when the snow
was here it covered
a lot of rubish,
It will be nice
to see it green
again, but hot
weather comes
with it
But we must not
cross the Bridge
till we get there,
Good by till we
meet again, Grandma
moses,

was glad to hear from
you and that you are.
happy that summer is
coming, But is it?
It froze the ground last
night,
But then the good Lord
has all wise given us seed
Time and harvest, and I don't
think he will turn us down
this Time
altho we are a wicked bunch
of people, fighting and killing
each other,
But I do hope it will soon
be over, then we can breath
in peace,

To O. K.—February 21, 1944

I like to finish of a painting
and then study it for a
week or 10 days, most allway
see then wher one can improve it,
and in regard to the size,
I have qust finished off 4
they were 40 by 35 in, realy to
large to be pretty,
But I would not like to
do any larger, as they are
to inconvenient,
Have qust layened away one
of my Dear friends on
wensday, now I must woork
to drown mememborys,
But it is Gods will,

To O. K.—March 4, 1944

Some one has asked me to
paint Biblical pictures,
and I say no I'll not paint.
some thing that we know
nothing about, might
qust as well paint some
thing that will happon 2
thousand years hence,

Feb 3. 1947.

Mr Otto Kallir Dear Sir,

I am sending you two small paintings that a nephew of mine has did,

He has no training what so ever, and this is his flirt attempt of this kind of woork.

Pleas express your opinion of his woork,

Don't hesitate to say what you think. should he continue? some one must take up the paint brush when I lay it down,

You will see the colors are not right, but now they are hard to find, Look them over and send them back,

Pleas,

To O. K.—April 14, 1947

It was very pretty day here but the next morning the Evergreens were bending down with snow,

To day it is not so warm here, a cold wind,

All are pretty well here, I have another Great-Grand son, that gives me eight " " Children,

I would love to see you all, but don't hurry as the roads are not very good yet and the country is not a bit pretty up here yet,

To H. B.—March 9, 1948

I tryed that interior but did not like it so I erased it, that dont seem to be in my line, I like to paint some thing that leads me on and on in to the unknown some thing that I want to see away on beyound well may be I try again,

Comment on an unfavorable write-up about which
Grandma Moses had just been informed.

Eagle Bridge n.y.
nov 11 1950.

Mr Dr Kallir Dear Friend, I hope your
are well this pretty day, it was snowing
This morning, but now warm and pretty,
I have been in bed all the pass week.,
with a sore throate and cold, but the
Dr let me sit up to day, so I think Ill be
all right soon,
Got your letter yesterday, am so sorry
your feel as you do about what people
say,
This is a free country and people
will talk, Let them, if we do what
is right they cant hurt us, and if
one gets a little ahead of another then
there is jealousy all,wise has been allwise
will be, and we must not pay any
attension to it, we must be above that,
now pleas dont worry about any thing as far
as I'm conserned for I am all right, have taken care of
my self for the pass 90 years and am good for austher,
Just take care of your self, and dont worry,
exsure penmenship this Time,
Best wishes for all,
Grandma moses,

It is snowing some, the Kidos had a nice tree, and wish you could see the mess this morning. I trust you are all well and geting along fine, The flowers are lovely and are growing more so. I have had a grand Chrismass, and now am in for a gay new years, wont they ever let me be, but it is all nice and they mean it for my good,

now here is Happ new year to you and all, may you have health and prosperity in all things, this coming year,

Grand ma Moses.

REPRODUCTIONS
OF SIXTEEN PAINTINGS
BY GRANDMA MOSES

SUGARING OFF
1938

From the collection of Mr. and Mrs. Albert D. Lasker, New York City

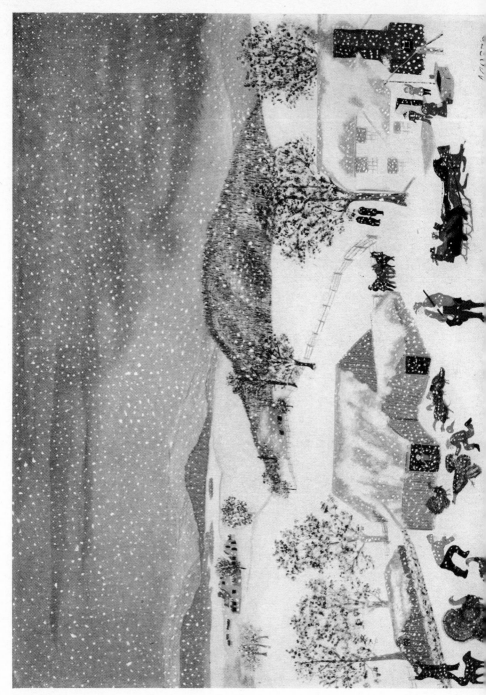

CATCHING THE
THANKSGIVING
TURKEY

MT. NEBO
IN WINTER
1943

THE OLD AUTOMOBILE

IN HARVEST TIME 1945

CHRISTMAS AT HOME

HOOSICK VALLEY
FROM MY WINDOW
1946

COVERED BRIDGE
1946

SNOWBALLING
1946

THUNDERSTORM
1948

THE QUILTING BEE